Billion Dollar Façade

The Rise And Fall Of Theranos And Elizabeth Holmes

Phil C. Senior

Bluesource And Friends

This book is brought to you by Bluesource And Friends, a happy book publishing company.

Our motto is **"Happiness Within Pages"**

We promise to deliver amazing value to readers with our books.

We also appreciate honest book reviews from our readers.

Connect with us on our Facebook page www.facebook.com/bluesourceandfriends and stay tuned to our latest book promotions and free giveaways.

Don't forget to claim your FREE books!

Brain Teasers:

https://tinyurl.com/karenbrainteasers

Harry Potter Trivia:

https://tinyurl.com/wizardworldtrivia

Sherlock Puzzle Book (Volume 2)

https://tinyurl.com/Sherlockpuzzlebook2

Also check out our best seller books

"67 Lateral Thinking Puzzles"

https://tinyurl.com/thinkingandriddles

"Rookstorm Online Saga"

https://tinyurl.com/rookstorm

omissions, or inaccuracies.

Table of Contents

Introduction

In the fall of 2015, *The Wall Street Journal* ran an article on its front page which effectively set the biotechnology world and the insular Silicon Valley scene on fire. Theranos, a much hailed startup which was disrupting the world of healthcare and led by a visionary young woman, was a fraud, the story claimed.

To most people, the article amounted to nothing short of blasphemy. To stain the reputation of Elizabeth Holmes and her company, valued at $10 billion, was to align oneself against progress and it was initially seen as the backward thinking that was prevalent in mainstream, non-Silicon Valley society. Here was the next Steve Jobs, right down to the ridiculous black turtleneck, being tarnished much in the manner Galileo was sabotaged by the Catholic Church for simply telling the truth.

The backlash from Theranos had followed similar lines of argument. The story was completely made up and the firm had rebuttals on hand which would disprove every single line of the story. The reporter who broke the story, John Carreyrou, had his name dragged through the mud and the journal was buried with threats of lawsuits from the powerful law firm representing Theranos.

However, despite the threats and vows to set things right, there was simply too much smoke around Theranos. It seemed as if the Valley had finally removed its blinders and began taking a look at facts. The facts were damning: Theranos and Elizabeth Holmes were frauds. As of current writing, Holmes and her crony are facing multiple charges of fraud and are battling to stave off jail time.

Most stories consist of all sorts of characters – good, bad, endearing and hateful. This story is not like that. Almost every person you will read about in this book is a fraud or behaves in an extremely stupid manner even when confronted with facts. There are no winners in this, just victims and the sociopathic perpetrators of fraud who still have the gall to go around behaving as if they are visionaries.

Elizabeth Holmes has never bothered to present facts to back her lofty claims. Instead, her only mode of operation has been to back a lofty story with an even loftier claim which paints her as the victim of an orchestrated plot. As you read in this book, you will realize that all of this is very much in her ballpark as far as her behavior goes.

Having never presented any sort of facts or detailed interviews of the same, this book relies heavily on the book *Bad Blood* by John Carreyrou, the same reporter who broke the story and faced a response from Holmes, which might have reminded him of how the mafia responded to threats.

This book also derives a lot of information from public news sources detailing events of Theranos' collapse and subsequent events. A lot of this story emanates from people who have worked for the corporation and were brave enough to speak out about the fraud that was being carried out. In doing so, they almost had their lives ruined and deserve every form of praise there is.

Due to the compartmentalized nature of how Theranos ran its operations, a lot of the information presented will not have a follow up to it simply because sources of such information themselves had no idea of a bigger picture. Holmes and her partner's strategy to deliberately keep everyone in the dark simply gave them more time to carry out their fraudulent scheme.

Billion Dollar Facade

Lastly, this is also a story of Silicon Valley hubris. A lot of the people involved in this story are extremely smart and intelligent, Holmes included. It is perfectly natural for such people to seek like company but in doing so, as this story shows, a lot gets lost and the echo chamber that results from this does far more damage than good.

Indeed, a major reason as to why Holmes has never publicly admitted to or shown any form of contrition for the fraud she perpetrated might be due to her adherence to the culture existent in Silicon Valley, right from the likes of Gates and Jobs to Zuckerberg and Kalanick.

Viewed in such a light, her only fault seems to be that she operated within the medical field and thus, the consequences of her following the culture which propped her up were very real, as opposed to a few malfunctioning lines of retail software and repeated ctrl+alt+deletes.

Either way, this is a story as old as Time, of a con artist misdirecting otherwise sensible people with shiny things while siphoning their money out of the back door. Those well versed with financial con artists will be reminded of the story of the South Sea Bubble when reading this. Indeed, the luminaries who ended up endorsing this fraud are no less exalted than those all those many centuries earlier.

Once again, I'd like to note that this book owes an immense amount to John Carreyrou's account from his book *Bad Blood* and his stories on the matter in the *Wall Street Journal*.

Chapter 1: Childhood

On February 3rd 1984, Noel Holmes, nee Daoust, gave birth to her first child, a girl named Elizabeth Anne Holmes in Washington D.C. Noel was a congressional staffer (Carreyrou, 2019) while her husband, Christian Holmes IV, held a number of posts in the State Department and other agencies.

While their financial position wasn't terribly exalted, the Holmes family was never more than middle to upper middle class; their social pedigree was nothing to sneeze at. Noel Holmes' father was a high ranking Pentagon official who was instrumental in turning the American army from a collection of draft-based recruits to a force made of volunteers. What's more, the family traced its origins all the way back to one of Napoleon's field generals.

If Noel was proud of her family's lineage, Christian was doubly so. The Holmes family traced its lineage back to Charles Louis Fleischmann, a Hungarian immigrant who made millions via his Fleischmann Yeast company. His daughter married a physician by the name of Christian Holmes and inherited her father's vast fortune. She was Elizabeth's great, great grandmother (Carreyrou, 2019).

The young couple never lacked for comfort thanks to Dr. Holmes' medical prowess and his father-in-law's political and financial connections. Eventually, Christian Holmes would go on to establish the Cincinnati General Hospital as well as the medical school at the University of Cincinnati.

The family's fortunes took a turn for the worse though, thanks to the profligacy of Christian II and Christian III, Elizabeth's great grandfather and grandfather respectively. This drain of wealth took its toll on Christian IV and led him to school his daughter on the greatness as well as the shortcomings of their family's background.

Christian IV was keenly aware of his family's history and was not hesitant to highlight its greatness. He was keen for his children, Elizabeth and Christian V, to not only live up to their exalted past but to also do good in the world via their efforts. These lessons were not lost on Elizabeth who, by all accounts, was an ambitious child.

Stanford And Houston

Christian's posts with the government led to the Holmes family living in Woodside, CA, which is a few miles down the road from Stanford's Palo Alto campus. While the exact years are not known, the Holmes family lived in that area around the late '80s, or when Elizabeth was around seven to ten years old.

Stanford at the time was already buzzing with the energy of the burgeoning computer industry and it so happened that the Holmes' neighbored with Tim Draper, a successful venture capitalist and a person who was considered one of the best venture capital investors in the valley. A third generation investor, Draper's daughter Betty and Elizabeth were close friends.

Billionaires And Monopoly

Christian travelled a fair bit thanks to his government posts, and one of his regular ports of call was Shanghai. This led to him becoming convinced of China's growing economic strength and he and Noel insisted on their children learning Mandarin. Thus, Elizabeth and Christian V (hereby referred to as Chris), ended up visiting China with their father as well as learning the language from a young age.

Elizabeth was an excellent student by all accounts and displayed an extremely competitive streak when it came to the things she wanted. When asked what her ambition was, a nine year old Elizabeth had a ready answer: To be a billionaire (Carreyrou, 2019). This wasn't the idle chat of a precocious child either, thanks to her father's ambition for his children to occupy the once uber wealthy status the Holmes family had.

The Holmes family often vacationed in Florida with Noel's brother Ron Dietz, and Elizabeth and her cousins often engaged in games of Monopoly. With her competitive streak in full flow, she would often beat her cousins at the game and sometimes made them play until she owned literally everything on the board. On one occasion when she lost, Elizabeth apparently ran right through her uncle's front screen door, unable to bear the thought of losing (Carreyrou, 2019).

Christian, meanwhile, was chafing at the ceiling his government job was placing on him and was actively seeking other opportunities in the private sector. The fact that he had two bright children who would eventually need support for college was not lost on him. Eventually, he accepted a position with the equipment maker Tenneco in Houston, around the time Elizabeth became a teenager.

High School

The Holmes children attended St. John's High School, a prestigious institution in Houston. High school was a tough transition for Elizabeth, like most people, and she wasn't particularly popular despite her good looks. Generally a shabby dresser and absorbed with whatever was going on inside her head, Elizabeth had a small social circle during her first year.

It's not known if any of this bothered her particularly at the time. Either way, the summer after her freshman year, Elizabeth applied to Stanford Summer School's Mandarin program. In what was an early display of her ability to charm anyone with her sincerity and intelligence, Elizabeth managed to talk her way into a program that was meant to be exclusively for college-age students.

The Holmes' were always consciously active on the social circuit and Elizabeth soon began dating the son of a prominent Houston surgeon during her sophomore year in high school. The summer program in Stanford seemed to ignite something in her and she soon hit the books, often studying till late and became a straight-A student.

Her ambition was clearly Stanford, and a lot of ideas which were running around in her head, of social and financial status combined with the need to do something great, were beginning to coalesce in her mind. Stanford provided the right opportunities for someone in her position, thanks to it's by now cemented reputation as a tech Mecca.

This was during the tech boom of the late '90s, and the dot-com crash notwithstanding, Stanford was abuzz with excitement. News of exciting startups dominated the scene and with the Valley's established venture capital ecosystem, funding was always available for those who were ambitious enough. At the time, the startup that was making the most noise was something called "Google".

Either way, it is easy to see the allure Stanford held for Elizabeth and in April 2002, she gained admission along with a $3000 President's grant to the college with the freedom to pursue studies in any field of her choice. This was great news for the Holmes family who were wading through rough times.

Christian had long since switched employers from Tenneco to Enron, the energy trading giant. The previous fall in 2001, the lid had been blown off the fraud Enron had engineered and Christian's financial position was shaky. In desperation, he turned to his old neighbor from Washington, Richard Fuisz, for advice. Fuisz was a successful businessman and while his relationship with Christian wasn't the warmest, he still cared enough to hear Christian out and give him advice.

Seeds Of A Row

While the relationship between the men wasn't the most cordial, their wives Noel and Lorraine got along extremely well, with both being a regular fixture at each other's homes. They were aware of the sour relationship between their husbands but never let it affect the both of them.

Christian, who was always a bit insecure about money, didn't like the way Fuisz flaunted his wealth. A licensed doctor, Fuisz had eventually gone into business by starting a company that manufactured medical films. He eventually sold this firm for $50 million and had a pretty high opinion of himself. In addition, he was also a prolific medical inventor and earned a sizeable income through royalties.

Compared to this Ferrari and Porsche driving businessman, Christian's government salary was a bit pathetic-looking, in his mind. Fuisz, for his part, was not the most reasonable character either. He had a reputation for keeping petty grudges and went to extreme lengths to exact revenge. More often than not, the magnitude of revenge was out of proportion with the perceived slight.

Fuisz, in his early days, was much more than a doctor. During the late '60s and '70s, he was also an undercover CIA operative, which seems like something straight out of Hollywood, but it is true. Either way, Fuisz was extremely active around the Middle East and had a vast network of contacts both within the government as well as the Arab league nations that comprised the region.

With his medical film business in full flow by this time, and with important clients in the Middle East, Fuisz personally received an offer of $53 million for his company from Vernon Loucks, the CEO of Baxter International. Fuisz accepted with the understanding that he would head Middle East operations for a period of at least three years.

However, shortly after the buyout, Fuisz was fired from his post for refusing to pay a bribe to a Saudi official in exchange for removing Baxter from the trading blacklist. This is, of course, Fuisz's claim and the truth of it cannot be verified. Either way, he sued Baxter and won $800,000 in a settlement. Here, Fuisz decided to take another slight to heart.

Loucks refused to shake Fuisz's hand during the signing of the settlement which infuriated the latter. Biding his time, he kept an eye on Baxter and noted with surprise the news of the company being taken off the blacklist by Syria. Reasoning that a bribe had been paid along with other shady dealings, Fuisz sent an agency operative to unearth some dirt around all of this.

It turned out that Baxter had promised Syria that they would cease all forms of investment in Israel, which put the firm directly in violation of American anti-boycott law. Fuisz faxed memos to the *Wall Street Journal* and the story hit Baxter with the force of a knockout punch, leading to Loucks' resignation.

Fuisz was no ordinary muckraker though. Through his son, he got in touch with the president of Yale's Jewish student body and convinced them to hold protests against the appointment of Loucks as a Yale trustee. Loucks promptly resigned and presumably Fuisz was finally satisfied.

This digression to paint the picture of the sort of man Richard Fuisz is will be relevant down the road. For now, all that needs to be kept in mind is that Christian Holmes was not to be blamed for his less than enthusiastic attitude towards Fuisz. As mentioned previously, there are very few heroes in this story and Fuisz is far from being one of them.

The Holmes remained in Houston while Elizabeth prepared to move to Palo Alto in order to attend Stanford. Christian established a small time consulting business which got them by and when Chris was admitted to Duke, Noel and Christian moved back to Washington D.C (around 2005), and the former re-established her friendship with Lorraine Fuisz.

Elizabeth, meanwhile, was fully ready to widen her horizons at Stanford. With lofty ideas of making the world a better place, thanks to Christian's exhortations, and with the ambition to become a billionaire, she duly arrived to college in the spring of 2002.

Chapter 2: A Vision

In seeking to make the world a better place, Elizabeth had a dual aim. While one can give her credit for the humanitarian aspect of this goal, the fact remains that the recognition she would receive played an important role as well to her. Elizabeth was not concerned with just being a billionaire, but also leaving her mark on the world.

The way she saw it, both of these goals went hand-in-hand. She had been brought up surrounded by pictures of Christian assisting and overseeing huge humanitarian efforts in Haiti and Cuba, among other war torn countries. Medical assistance formed an extremely important part of these projects and in biotechnology; Elizabeth spotted a perfect amalgam of a profitable industry and the ability to be recognized for humanitarianism.

She shortly enrolled into Stanford's chemical engineering program.

First Mentors And Connections

Channing Robertson looked nothing like his fifty-nine years of age and was often spotted around the campus in leather jackets which further ingratiated him to his students. The head of the university's chemical engineering program, Robertson had been teaching at Stanford since the '70s.

Shortly after conducting a seminar on controlled drug delivery devices, a burgeoning field within the bio-tech space, he was approached by Elizabeth Holmes and was immediately impressed by both her intelligence and her sincerity. She had taken his introductory course to chemical engineering as well and soon convinced him to allow her to help out with his research projects (Carreyrou, 2019).

It so happened that Robertson had a Ph.D. student working on a project to determine the best enzymes for laundry detergents and referred Elizabeth to him. The Ph.D. student, Shaunak Roy, was equally impressed with Elizabeth, and despite her young age, soon came to view her as an equal. This is especially remarkable considering that Holmes was still a college freshman at this point.

She was equally active socially as she was academically, dating a sophomore student JT Batson (Carreyrou, 2019), and adjusted quite well to campus life. Batson, for his part, found Elizabeth quite polished and worldly despite her age. He did note that she seemed very guarded and wasn't someone who opened up too much.

Holmes' insatiable ambition soon began to assert itself and perhaps this is where she first began to form ideas in her head which would enable her to change the biotech field she had set her eyes on. Over the winter break after her first semester, she openly discussed her lack of enthusiasm with regards to pursuing a Ph.D. and reiterated her desire to make lots of money (Carreyrou, 2019).

The result of all this was Batson receiving a knock on his door during the following Spring semester and Elizabeth informing him that she just didn't have time to spare for him, now that she was planning on starting a company. Presumably the fact that he was dumped for a company, as opposed to another man, softened the blow for Batson. Either way, it's quite clear that by this time, Holmes was planning on dropping out of Stanford.

That summer, she landed an internship at the prestigious genome institute in Singapore and her experience there would lead her to finalize the vision she had in her mind all this while.

A Plan

2003 saw large parts of Asia hit by a virus called SARS (severe acute respiratory syndrome). A considerable amount of Holmes' work at the institute was to test patient samples obtained from syringes and nasal swabs (Carreyrou, 2019). While these old timey methods were reliable when it came to the delivery of samples, she also noted the fact that testing them and prescribing medicine took longer, thanks to the inefficiency of the whole process.

All in all, it seemed like there was an opening for a solution that would ease the collection of samples as well as enable doctors to diagnose and prescribe medicine as quickly as possible. Just to make it clear, such ideas were not unique at the time and within a few years, companies would release market-ready solutions.

These solutions did not turn out to be ground-breaking thanks to the fact that such technology could not translate medical necessities very well. For example, depending on the type of tests to be conducted, patient sample sizes differed, which is why ultimately, a syringe and needle was the preferred way to collect blood and other samples.

Holmes, though, was not privy to industry data and given her young age, perhaps her arrogance can be excused. After all, it is exactly such ignorance that fuels great creation. Either way, she returned to the US with a head full of ideas. Her first stop was her parents' house in Houston where she immediately threw herself into the task of putting her vision on paper.

Noel later recalled (Carreyrou, 2019) that Elizabeth stayed up for five days, sleeping as little as one or two hours a night and subsisting on trays of food Noel bought for her. This sort of work ethic was something the Holmes were used to from their daughter, right since her second year of high school. The time eventually came for Elizabeth to head back to Stanford and she managed to catch up on some sleep in her mother's car.

The net result of all her work was a patent application for a wearable device that would diagnose and treat medical conditions. In the shape of an arm patch, this device was the first iteration of the product that would eventually form a part of Theranos' fraudulent vision.

As mentioned earlier, Holmes was not exactly up-to-date on the inner workings of the medical device industry, and given his reaction, we can safely presume that Channing Robertson wasn't either. He professed himself impressed with the details Holmes had devoted to the design and was convinced that the idea could be translated to reality. In addition, he was the first person to fall victim to Holmes' enthusiasm and seemingly magnetic personality.

For all her faults, Holmes was and is an incredible salesperson and it is easy to imagine Robertson buying into her vision. Besides, he had hardly ever encountered a student as driven and ambitious as Elizabeth, and as such, had no qualms encouraging her to go after her plans. The only skeptic in all of this was Shaunak Roy.

Roy, raised in Chicago and the son of Indian immigrants, was more practical by nature and considered the whole thing a bit unrealistic. However, when faced with the dual pressure of Holmes' ambition and Robertson's enthusiastic endorsement, he relented and came on board with the idea of floating a startup to produce the device.

Thus, in May 2004, Real Time Cures Inc. was launched, with

Elizabeth Holmes controlling a majority stake and Shaunak Roy a minority participant. In addition, Channing Robertson joined the company as an adviser. In what would be a harbinger of things to come, the company's earliest paychecks bore the name "Real Time Curses" thanks to a typo (Carreyrou, 2019).

Holmes dropped out of Stanford shortly after starting the company.

Beginnings

While anyone can start a company, running it and helping it realize its vision is another matter. Holmes and Roy were met with a dash of cold, hard reality soon after they launched it in the form of the offices they could afford to lease. While technically in Menlo Park, the company's first offices were on the wrong side of the tracks, in a place more famous for its murder rate than ground-breaking biotech.

Holmes soon got to work, taping her family's extensive network and leveraging her, not inconsiderable, charm. The first investor to come on board was Tim Draper, father of Jesse, Holmes' childhood friend. Draper, being a successful venture capitalist, added a massive layer of credibility to the new company, now rechristened "Theranos", an amalgam of therapy and diagnostics.

With $1 million in the bank from Draper, Holmes turned her attention to Christian's long time friend, the corporate turnaround specialist Victor Palmieri. Palmieri and Christian had known each other since their government days and the former was instantly impressed with the audacity and determination with which Holmes laid out her vision.

Holmes' initial pitch to investors was a twenty-six page document

(Carreyrou, 2019) which contained the details of a device dubbed the "TheraPatch". Combining micro and nano technology, the patch would draw blood painlessly through micro needles and the blood would be analyzed by a microchip sensing system. This system would then recommend the amount of drugs the patient needed to be delivered and via a wireless system, would transmit the results to the patient's doctor.

While the idea of nanotechnology as applied to drawing blood and other technological components is more than realistic, the fact remains that the blood being drawn cannot be downsized to a nano size. After all, since entire human beings cannot be shrunk, the amount of blood required for a diagnosis cannot shrink. For whatever reason, this fact appears to have escaped the notice of investors and Holmes was able to explain this away under the catch-all umbrella of "nanotech".

Not everyone was on board with this Alice in Wonderland thinking. During one of her presentations to a VC fund named MedVenture associates, Holmes was visibly rattled (Carreyrou, 2019). MedVenture specialized in medical technology investment and they pointed out that the microchip sensing system was already commercialized by a firm named Abaxis. Abaxis' version could not perform what Holmes had in mind, so how exactly did she plan on delivering what was being promised? Holmes walked out of that meeting after an hour.

Despite these setbacks, Holmes managed to charm $6 million into Theranos' coffers from prestigious investors like John Bryan, a venture capitalist, and Stephen Feinberg, a board member of the MD Anderson Cancer Center in Houston. In addition, some members of her family like her aunt Elizabeth Dietz contributed as well.

Billion Dollar Facade

The Hottest Start Up In The Valley

While all this was going on, Shaunak Roy began to see that none of this was practically possible. He managed to convince Holmes of the fact that the medication recommendation portion of the patch was completely unworkable and that Theranos was best served by sticking to the diagnostic part.

They soon discovered that, thanks to the patch design of the product, even this was implausible and that they needed a better design which could be bigger in size but also portable enough so as to be easily carried around. Holmes' vision for this product was something similar to the blood glucose readers used by diabetic patients. With such devices, the patient pricks their finger for a drop of blood and the device spits back a blood sugar level number.

Holmes wanted the Theranos device to perform far more tests than just a blood sugar analysis though, and eventually, she and Shaunak arrived at a cartridge and reader system. The patient would prick their finger for a small drop of blood and place it into the credit card-sized cartridge. The cartridge would then be placed inside the reader and pumps in the reader would force the blood to flow through tiny tubes within the cartridge.

These tubes would have filters which would separate the plasma in the blood and direct it to tiny receptacles which housed antibodies. The reaction of the plasma to the antibodies would be read by the device and transmitted wirelessly to the doctor, thereby enabling them to adjust their patients' medication instantly.

By fall of 2005, Theranos had grown to 25 employees and had a working prototype, dubbed "Theranos 1.0" (Carreyrou, 2019) and a sound business plan whereby they would lease the devices to pharmaceutical companies in order to monitor reactions during clinical trials. Shaunak Roy was finally optimistic about the whole thing and Theranos was attracting quite a lot of buzz, thanks to Holmes' charisma and enthusiasm.

All in all, things were looking great.

Chapter 3: First Cracks

Now that the prototype was fully ready, all that remained to be done was to create a working device, a "minimum viable product" in VC speak, to show to investors and potential clients. Theranos jumped into this with all the enthusiasm it could muster, in addition to expanding its staff.

The roster at Theranos read like a who's who of Silicon Valley. The chairman of the board by this time was Donald Lucas, the investor who had mentored Larry Ellison and had taken Oracle public. Ellison himself was an investor in Theranos. In charge of bioinformatics was Tim Kemp, who had over thirty years' worth of experience with IBM. The SVP of products, John Howard, was a notable alumnus of Panasonic's chip making division. In addition, there was Diane Parks who had over twenty-five year's worth of experience in the biotech industry.

Then there was the CFO, Henry Mosley who had begun his career first with Intel and had then run the finances of four valley companies and was generally amongst the most respected financial executives in the industry. All this collection of talent was unusual at a regular company in the valley, let alone a two-year-old startup. At the center of it all was the twenty-two year old CEO who everyone looked up to.

Mosley would be one of the first casualties of Elizabeth Holmes' dislike of the truth.

Building An MVP

In early 2006, another valley standout was being interviewed by Holmes for the position of engineering head. Edmond Ku, or Ed as he was called, was a veteran and was generally the go-to guy for all matters engineering for a valley startup. From the outside, Ku wasn't quite sure what to make of this company located on the wrong side of the tracks in Menlo Park yet boasting such an impressive roster (Carreyrou, 2019).

Then there was the founder who was a college dropout and had no training whatsoever in biology, chemistry or technology and yet, here she was, running a biotech firm. Ku's background was in electronics engineering and not in medical devices, so he was skeptical about the whole thing.

His doubts were dispelled though, when Holmes began to talk about her vision. The instances of 100,000 Americans who died every year from adverse reactions to drugs would not occur anymore. Theranos would help pharmaceutical companies keep drugs on the market that were vital to alleviate patient suffering but at the moment had to be withdrawn thanks to side effects from higher than required doses.

Theranos' mission wasn't to just build a device. It was to change the world and make it a better place. Coming from the innocent looking, idealistic twenty-two year old sitting across the table from him, all of this seemed possible. Ku was sold completely.

However, he couldn't help but wonder at the startlingly deep voice Holmes had, almost as if it was an affectation.

Challenges

The first shock Ku received was that the Theranos 1.0 was a hit or miss product, mostly a miss. The prototype by itself was nowhere near the final version the product had to have and despite this, it worked sporadically and never really managed to provide reliable results. However in valley startups, this sort of thing was quite normal and like most valley veterans, Ku had signed up for the challenge.

And what a challenge it was. Thanks to a professed fear of needles, Holmes had insisted on the amount of blood that needed to be drawn to be minuscule. This posed the first challenge for Ku. Given the microscopic amount of blood drawn, it would need to be diluted with a saline solution in order for it to flow through the cartridge, pass through the filters and arrive at the receptacles containing the antibodies.

Naturally, diluting an already small amount of blood was not ideal but Ku was not in charge of the chemistry. This was his second challenge. Holmes' idiosyncratic style of management meant that teams were not encouraged to communicate with one another and thus, any failure that happened left Ku wondering whether it was an issue with his engineering side of things or whether the chemistry didn't work.

Yet another challenge was that aside from the saline/blood solution, the cartridge needed to house tiny portions of liquids called "reagents" which would help deliver a signal once the plasma reacted with the antibodies. Release the reagents too soon and the entire cartridge would have to be replaced. Costing over $200 a pop, this was an expensive mistake to make.

Despite all of this and his growing frustration with Holmes' absurd management style, Ku and his team soldiered on, acutely aware that Theranos had burned through its initial $6 million in funding and would soon need more money to be injected if things were to continue.

Raising Money

Like any Silicon Valley startup worth its salt, Theranos and Elizabeth Holmes considered making money a secondary objective when it came to business. After all, who has time for money when you're changing the world? She wasn't particularly fussed about the need to raise a second round of funding, which was virtually guaranteed thanks to the pedigree she had on board. Theranos eventually raised $8 million from its investors.

At the third stage, however, all startups needed to show some form of customer engagement and interest for the product. The only product Theranos had as of now was the 1.0, which was a malfunctioning prototype. With the board expecting drafts of contracts from big pharmaceutical companies, Holmes needed to work something out soon.

With Ku and his engineering team still struggling to get the cartridges working, Holmes devised a plan to achieve her ends. By November 2006, Theranos had meetings set up with companies such as Novartis in Switzerland and Holmes and a clutch of team members flew to the company headquarters for a presentation.

Prior to the meeting, Holmes had tasked Mosley, the CFO, to prepare financial projections which, according to Mosley (Carreyrou, 2019), bordered on optimistic but was par for course with valley startups. As such, Mosley wasn't terribly concerned with being too optimistic because as far as he knew, the prototype worked and he had no idea of what Ku and his team were up to.

Holmes segregated every single area of the company in the name of trade secrecy, to keep anyone except herself from knowing the extent of progress with the company's products. Thus, senior management like Mosley had no idea of what was actually happening. Either way, the presentation seemed to go well and employees received an email from Tim Kemp, deeming the whole thing a success.

An email from Holmes soon followed, declaring that Novartis was on board and that a commercial contract was on the way. Mosley had heard of a number of commercial contracts being underway, but absurdly, hadn't actually seen any of them. Holmes managed to separate her CFO from sales contracts and had managed to convince him that they were under legal review.

It's hard to believe that an experienced hand like Mosley could have allowed himself to be hoodwinked like this, but one must make allowances for Holmes' charisma after all. Either way, once the team returned from Switzerland, he noticed everyone seemed downbeat, in marked contrast to Holmes' demeanor. Mosley couldn't understand the reason for the gloom on the team members' part (Carreyrou, 2019).

Knowing full well the embargo on departments interacting with one another, Mosley snuck around and found Shaunak Roy who he figured, as Holmes' partner, would know what was going on.

Turnover

Roy was initially reluctant but eventually let Mosley know that the 1.0 had not worked as planned. Mosley was taken aback by this since he assumed the system had always worked. After all, when investors came over to view the system at Theranos' offices, it always worked.

In what was a bigger shock to him, Roy then revealed that the system setup in the office was a fake. While the blood flowing through the cartridge was real, the result was almost sure to never arrive. Thus, Holmes and Roy had pre-recorded a signal and transmitted that to the investors in order to make it seem like the device worked. The team had pulled this exact stunt at Novartis as well.

This was outright fraud and Mosley was deeply uncomfortable with this. However, he wasn't overly alarmed or outraged by this because selling a defective initial product was common in Silicon Valley startups. Larry Ellison famously sold defective copies of Oracle software to his clients and used the money from those sales to push better, patched products back to those customers. Microsoft initially followed the same policy as well.

What made Mosley a tad anxious was the fact that this was not a few lines of code but potentially, medical results being tampered with. With his ears now pricked up, he proceeded to his scheduled meeting with Holmes, fully making up his mind to question her about all of this. After all, if the contracts were based on fake results and if the funding, which Theranos had just received to the tune of $32 million, was based on these contracts, surely the company was perpetrating a fraud upon its investors?

Mosley's meeting started off pleasantly enough. He soon brought up the topic of the tests failing and Holmes brushed it aside as something that could easily be fixed. Given that Roy had just painted a very different picture, Mosley didn't let the matter go and suggested that they stop the demos until the issue was fixed and that they would have to revise the numbers downward to reflect reality better. Holmes' smile and cheery demeanor vanished instantly.

Next thing he knew, Mosley was asked to sign an NDA and was escorted out of the building by security without the chance to gather his personal belongings, thus ending Henry Mosley's misbegotten adventure with Theranos. Still, he was one of the lucky ones (Carreyrou, 2019).

Survival Of The Fittest

While Henry Mosley was having his title stripped off him, Edmond Ku and his team continued to toil away at the cartridges, forever bumping up against the restrictions Holmes placed on them. He noticed the constant turnover of staff and noted that Mosley was soon gone as well. A rumor spread around the office that the former CFO was caught embezzling funds.

Ku wasn't too flustered about this since Theranos had just raised $32 million in its third round of funding. As long as the money was present, he reasoned that any problems could be worked out. Soon after this, he received a visit from Holmes who was visibly upset and demanded that he run his team on a 24/7/365 basis – in other words, without breaks.

Given the already long hours his team was putting in, Ku pushed back and this irritated Holmes even more. Dismissing concerns of burnout by suggesting she could always hire more engineers, Holmes walked away from Ku, and that was the beginning of the end for the head of the engineering department.

Soon, Ku noticed engineers were being hired without his knowledge and separate teams were being formed. Eventually, Tony Nugent, who had spent his previous eleven years at Logitech, came to head this new upstart team. Nugent was initially hired as a consultant by the VP of product development at Theranos before the guy who hired him ended up being fired after working for just six months.

Edison

Holmes and Roy's initial vision for the Theranos testing system was based on microfluidics. The principle underlying everything Ku was working on was based on this theory. Nugent's first act upon arrival was to promptly abandon it on the grounds that he simply could not see how it could be made to work.

Holmes, by this point, was willing to revise her vision, which had gone from a patch to a microfluid-based cartridge, to a device that could be placed in a patient's home and carried around easily. Thus, reasoning that he had more size to work with, Nugent got busy. The first thing he did was to purchase a commercial glue dispensing robot called the Fisnar.

This robot was pretty rudimentary but it allowed Nugent to realize his vision for the product. Instead of focusing on the revolutionary aspects of it, Nugent sought to focus on the value addition their product could provide by replicating the actions of bench chemists. Thus, by sealing everything in a black box, Theranos would reduce the time required to process blood test results.

In order to focus on delivering results, which was a problem the 1.0 was plagued with, Nugent sought to have the new machine master a process known as Chemiluminescent Immunoassay. In this type of blood testing, used to detect a few symptoms, the reagents are mixed with the plasma and the antibodies, and this results in an output of light. The degree of brightness of the light emitted reveals underlying symptoms.

The 1.0 cartridge was modified by making it slightly bigger in size and having it contain just two tubes and two pipette tips. Pipettes are simply slender pipes used to extract and transport small amounts of fluid. The blood sample, which was now 50 microlitres in size up from the 10 microlitres Ku was slaving over, was poured into one of the tubes. The other tube contained a saline diluting solution.

This cartridge was placed into the black box, which was slightly smaller than a desktop CPU, and the robot arm inside mixed the saline solution with the blood via the first pipette. Then, it transported this diluted blood onto the second pipette which was coated with antibodies. Lastly, reagents were released onto this mixture and the resulting light was measured.

This is how Theranos managed to get its first working product. Holmes decided to christen it the "Edison". Its development was just as well because Holmes had pressed forward and had begun testing the 1.0 on cancer patients in a clinic in Tennessee, fully knowing that the system did not work and was fake. Once the Edison was working, Holmes promptly began showing it off to investors and the like.

Nugent was deeply uncomfortable with this due to the product not being fully tested. The extent of this is shown by the fact that he didn't know which warning stickers were appropriate for the product. With the legal department being of no help, Nugent did his own research and eventually slapped a few rudimentary stickers onto it

(Carreyrou, 2019).

Shortly after, Edmond Ku was summoned by HR and was told that his services were no longer required. Nugent was gracious enough to call him a taxi to transport him back home, something neither HR nor Holmes bothered with (Carreyrou, 2019).

Another Exit

The constant turnover, the paranoid secrecy, and the recent pivot from a path breaking microfluidic system to a less complex glue robot dispensing black box, proved too much for Shaunak Roy to take. Smart enough to stay on Holmes' good side, he notified her of his intention to return to university and his lack of interest in the venture now that microfluids were abandoned.

Holmes wasn't too bothered by this. As far as she could see, Theranos finally had a working product and the valuation of the company, already at an absurd $145 million, was only going to go up. This didn't stop her from applying the screws to Roy, though, the farewell party she threw for him notwithstanding.

Roy agreed to sell his 1.13 million shares back to Holmes at an 80% discount from the price at which the previous valuation was recorded (Carreyrou, 2019). Given the progress of the Edison, the real discount would have been at least double that. However, one cannot fault Holmes for this decision in any way since it appears to be a purely business minded one. After all, Roy was equally happy to walk away with a payout of $565,000.

Either way, along with Roy went the last vestige of sanity at the top of Theranos. While not completely blameless himself, Roy was willing to confront the problems at the company and managed to steer Holmes down more reasonable paths most of the time. Besides, as long as Roy was present, Theranos did not engage in any sort of behavior that was too far out of the ordinary for a valley startup.

With this last restraint gone, Holmes was free to bring in someone who would push her further down the path of insanity and make every Theranos employee's life a living hell.

Chapter 4: The Rise And Rise Of Theranos

Whatever the nature of the cracks that were already appearing at Theranos, none of this was visible from the outside. By 2007, right around the time the iPhone was being released, Elizabeth Holmes was being lauded as the model entrepreneur of her generation.

Theranos, while not yet popular in the mainstream media, had already attracted a huge following within valley circles and everyone was lining up to get a piece of the pie. Holmes, for her part, enjoyed the attention she was getting and was outwardly committed to changing the world, as she repeatedly outlined in her public statements.

Things were very different on the inside, though, both with Holmes and Theranos.

Motivation

Elizabeth Holmes doesn't think of herself as someone ordinary to this day. This might be justified to some extent, given her unquestionable intelligence and the size of her vision. Holmes, right from the start, saw herself as the next Steve Jobs and idolized what he was doing at Apple at the time.

Indeed, during her investor pitches, Holmes dubbed the 1.0 the "iPod of healthcare" and her vision to place Theranos' products in the homes of people was much in line with what Jobs had in mind. Holmes even went as far as to paste a quote from one of her mentors, Channing Robertson, where he mentioned her as being the next Steve Jobs or Bill Gates, overhead in her office.

While Jobs and Gates were motivated by the dual need to make great products as well as make money, in Holmes' case there was almost no desire to actually make a great product. Despite her lofty words, her actions have repeatedly borne out this fact. All in all, she was and is far more concerned with projecting a certain image than actually living it, aside from becoming really rich of course.

Obsessed with being taken as a serious entrepreneur, she decided to adopt a heavier, deeper tone of voice which Edmond Ku had previously noticed. Holmes went to great lengths to adopt this obviously fake voice. Given her pedigree though, most people brushed it aside as a harmless quirk. There is no doubt that in the male dominated environs of Silicon Valley, she must have felt some pressure to be taken seriously as one of the few female entrepreneurs.

However, given the list of her backers and the people she had working for her, one wonders at the need to prolong such theatrics. With the release of the iPhone, which coincided with Theranos raising a third round of funding, Holmes was ready to take her company to bigger stages.

Her first step was to begin to imitate Apple by hiring its employees.

The Board Member

Avie Tevanian had heard a lot about Theranos when a headhunter approached him with the prospect of becoming one of the directors of the board at the company. Tevanian, a veteran of NeXT, Steve Jobs' venture in the '80s, and the former head of software engineering at Apple, was one of Jobs' closest friends, to the extent that Jobs had any friends.

The work at Apple had tired him out and by this point in time, with more money than he knew what to do with, Tevanian had settled into a quiet life, spending time with his wife and kids. He considered the Theranos offer mostly because he was intrigued by what people were saying about Holmes and, of course, the army of prestigious mentors and backers she had (Carreyrou, 2019).

Tevanian soon became one of them after meeting with Holmes. She sold him on the vision she had for Theranos, about how she wanted to change the world. This time, her pitch even included stuff about building disease maps based on the data Theranos would collect and how the company could predict the occurrence of cancer based on mathematical models. Being a pretty typical valley executive, Tevanian ate it up and soon joined the board by purchasing $1.6 million worth of shares.

While his initial meetings as part of the board went well, Tevanian couldn't help but look at what was going on right in front of his face. Perhaps his lack of prior proximity to Holmes enabled him to question things better. He noticed that the promises of ever-larger revenues that Holmes kept promising never materialized. Holmes mentioned a cancer patient study that Theranos was involved in Tennessee that was about to result in Pfizer coming on board with the Edison.

We've already seen what this study was and how it was conducted thanks to Edmond Ku's experiences. This is a repeated pattern with Holmes where a dubious study or source is wildly exaggerated and thanks to her charisma and salesmanship, she largely managed to hoodwink everyone around her. Tevanian, this time, was not completely sold but nonetheless didn't raise a fuss. However, he soon had an opportunity to raise a protest against Holmes and in the process, got to see a darker pattern of actions which revealed her to be the sociopath that she actually is (Carreyrou, 2019).

Holmes proposed to the board's compensation committee, via the chairman Don Lucas, that she wanted to create a foundation for tax planning purposes and that the committee would have to approve a special grant of stock to it. Tevanian saw this as the poorly disguised attempt to wrest voting control for the stock from the board it was. Lucas, however, treated Holmes with an almost sycophantic reverence and clearly thought of her as another Steve Ellison, whom Lucas had mentored in the past.

Accordingly, Tevanian raised an objection, the sole member to do so. Tevanian had been getting increasingly vocal at board meetings asking for the commercial contracts that Holmes kept touting and asking increasingly uncomfortable questions about the delays with the Edison. Such questions are routine for board members to ask, but not in Holmes' world.

Either way, Tevanian received a message from Lucas mentioning that Holmes felt he was being disruptive. Tevanian retaliated by meeting Lucas with material that he felt justified his case and that he felt Holmes, while enthusiastic, needed some adult supervision in order to move Theranos forward.

Lucas' reply was to ask Tevanian to resign. What's more, he needed to forfeit his rights to purchase more stock, including the shares of the recently departed Shaunak Roy. Tevanian was shocked at the resignation request and was outraged at what he clearly saw were strong arm tactics being used to crush his dissenting voice.

The firm's legal counsel, Michael Esquivel, soon got in touch with Tevanian and thus began a barrage of threats from Theranos. The company threatened to sue Tevanian for breach of his fiduciary duties and for making false public statements about the company. These accusations seemed straight out of lalaland as far as Tevanian was concerned, since he hadn't done any such thing.

It was clear to him that Holmes was the one doing the taking through the company's lawyer and the speed and ferocity with which she was reacting to a perceived slight disturbed him. The difference between the person doing the talking now and the wide eyed young woman, who idolized Steve Jobs during their first meeting, was stark.

There was also the arrogance behind the accusations of a lawsuit. At this point in time, Tevanian's personal net worth was far greater than Theranos'. If he wanted to, he could have bankrupted the firm and this fact was clearly lost on Holmes thanks to her exaggerated sense of importance.

Either way, Tevanian wanted no part of Theranos anymore and duly resigned and signed whatever papers Theranos sent him. Most of all, he was shocked at the extent to which experienced investors like Lucas had been duped by Holmes. In a final letter to the board, Tevanian warned them of the lengths to which Holmes would seek retribution against someone who wasn't 100% with her (Carreyrou, 2019).

The letter was presumably binned by Lucas and his blinkered associates.

Secrets And Paranoia

If Tevanian was the first Apple transplant to Theranos, Ana Arriola was a close second. Indeed, she followed Tevanian's lead to Theranos, being similarly swept up in the initial flush of meeting someone as charismatic as Holmes. Arriola received the same spiel as Tevanian did, about the disease maps and cancer prediction models that Theranos wanted to build, and couldn't help but be impressed at the scale of the vision the young, bubbly woman in front of her was laying out.

Arriola noted the reverence Holmes had for Steve Jobs and as the chief product architect at Theranos, she saw the extent to which Holmes wanted the Edison to replicate the iMac. The Edison's outer case was to be dual colored like the iMac and it needed to have a touchscreen interface like the iPhone.

There was the problem of concealing the noise the arm inside the case made but given that it wasn't too loud, Arriola didn't see this as a major concern. There was an initial design of the case floating around, designed by the famed industrial designer Yves Behar no less. Nugent and his team were already discovering the impracticality of this design but Arriola wasn't aware of any of this as of yet.

Arriola was also responsible for what would eventually become Holmes' trademark look. Suggesting that, since she admired Jobs so much, it wouldn't be a bad idea to give herself a makeover along the lines of the legendary founder of Apple. Holmes, from that day on, took to wearing a black turtleneck and black slacks and in a typical move, later claimed she had always loved black turtlenecks.

Joining Arriola was Justin Maxwell who was recruited to work on the UX and UI portion of the Edison's software system. In addition, he was also in charge of developing the look and feel of the Edison's cartridges. Maxwell and Arriola were among the more prominent transplants from Apple.

It wasn't long before they received the full blast of Theranos' paranoid work culture, which was in stark contrast to Apple or any other firm. For starters, there was the strange no communication rule which existed between departments. Information was so tightly segregated that employees couldn't even message each other due to the fear of trade secrets being leaked. Shortly before this, Holmes had dreamed up a case of industrial espionage involving the 1.0 and Theranos was involved in a vindictive lawsuit against three former employees (which it would later settle).

Never mind the fact that the 1.0 rarely worked; to Holmes the mere fact that her employees had dared speak to one another about Theranos' product was nothing short of betrayal. As illustrated by the high staff turnover rate, the work atmosphere at Theranos was somewhere between stifling and oppressive.

The head of IT, a man by the name of Matt Bissel, was the guard dog for all of this. Employees were forbidden from plugging in USB sticks and one employee was fired on the spot for doing so (Carreyrou, 2019). While this policy isn't extraordinary by itself, the decision to fire someone instantly for a first time violation is.

Maxwell had the distinct impression Holmes had instructed Bissel and his team to actively snoop on the employees. It was a regular occurrence for members of the IT team to approach employees with faux friendly tones in order to get them to rat on others within the organization. Holmes' personal assistants would even friend other employees on Facebook and report back to her the contents of their posts (Carreyrou, 2019).

Billion Dollar Facade

This paranoia would hit record levels when the board would convene for meetings at the office. Employees were strictly forbidden from even making eye contact with the board members and had to appear busy. The meetings themselves were conducted behind closed doors and the windows were covered with screens. All in all, a model workplace Theranos was not.

Arriola meanwhile was coming to terms with all of this and noted with rising unease the extreme nature to which Holmes took everything. She noticed how Holmes was the friendliest person in the world as long as you agreed with everything she said but could turn cold in an instant, much like how Henry Mosley had found out.

The CFO position was still vacant despite more than a year passing from the time of Mosley's departure for rumored embezzlement. Rumors were a natural by-product of this strict workplace. Arriola had heard news of how Nugent's engineering team and the chemistry team were not on speaking terms and of how commercial contracts were constantly stuck in legal review.

Even more alarming was the sudden departure of Tevanian, whom she knew personally, and now there was a rumor circulating of how he was disrupting the company's goals and had threatened Holmes. Arriola knew this to be a bald-faced lie, having worked with Tevanian and witnessed his almost teddy bear-like nature (Carreyrou, 2019).

The final nail in the coffin was when she learned of the study conducted on cancer patients using the old 1.0 equipment and of how these results were being used to market Theranos' supposed effectiveness in administering correct doses of drugs. With her relationship with Holmes already on edge, Arriola bit the bullet and confronted Holmes about the malfunctioning equipment.

Holmes' reaction, predictably, was to ask Arriola whether she wanted to be a part of the organization moving forward (Carreyrou, 2019). This shocked Arriola but as we have seen thus far, this sort of thing was completely par for course for Holmes. Arriola ended up quitting her job by day's end, not able to stand the secrecy and paranoia that surrounded Holmes.

New Digs

To the public eye, Theranos was climbing higher than ever. The company was now conservatively valued, in 2008, at around $200 million, with exact figures not being available thanks to it being a private corporation. Holmes, for her part, was embracing her rising celebrity and was a regular feature in insider valley publications like Red Herring magazine.

Given the growing stature of the company, it was appropriate that Theranos find new headquarters. Its existing East Palo Alto location was no place most venture capitalist investors would be caught dead being seen in. The company eventually decided on a pricey piece of real estate on Hillview Avenue in Palo Alto.

A stone's throw from the Stanford campus and around the corner from HP's headquarters, the move was a strong signal of Theranos' growing prosperity. The company's investors viewed it as the crown jewel of their investments. This was the time when the theme of disruption was still in its infancy and hadn't quite hit the mainstream as of yet. Uber would eventually do that a few years later.

For now, though, the existing theme of all investments in the valley centered around changing the world order. As a result, anything which even had a whiff of disruption ended up getting funded. Indeed, the formula to getting rich on paper was simple at this time: Enroll yourself in Stanford, poke around for a few investors, include a few keywords like "disruptive", "world changing", "global scale" and "exponential growth", and you have yourself a Series A funded startup.

Holmes ticked all of these boxes and managed to work around her lack of a degree thanks to her family's social connections and her considerable charisma. Either way, Theranos was on the up and the job of coordinating the move fell to the much maligned head of IT and security, Matt Bissel.

Further Changes

Bissel was painted by large sections of Theranos' employees as the villain but in reality, all he was doing was following Holmes' orders. In fact, he was just as frustrated and puzzled by his boss' behavior as the others (Carreyrou, 2019). His job by this time, in early 2008, spanned both IT as well as security and when the time came to coordinate the move, he found himself once again squarely at odds with Holmes.

Bissel had managed to stay on Holmes' good side until this point by enforcing what he saw were justifiable security measures. A lot of Silicon Valley companies jealously guarded their intellectual property and given the breadth of Theranos' vision, this sort of secrecy seemed reasonable to Bissel. His first misgivings occurred with the dismissal of Mosley as the CFO.

Mosley had, unfortunately, downloaded pornography on his work laptop and Holmes retroactively used this as a justification to fire him. Thus, the rumor around Theranos regarding Mosley changed from embezzlement to downloading porn. However idiotic Mosley was, the fact remained clear to Bissel that he wasn't fired for this reason but for something unconnected. Bissel had a feeling it was due to getting on Holmes' bad side.

He soon found this out for himself. When Holmes discovered that Theranos would owe a month's rent if they didn't vacate their old premises by midnight at the end of the month, she frantically called Bissel and ordered him to postpone the move date by almost two weeks. This led to Bissel, comically, being told by the moving company that their workforce was unionized, code for "controlled by the mob", and that changing companies would lead to negative consequences.

None of this mattered to the budding "next Steve Jobs" however, and Bissel found himself repeatedly shot down, no matter the size of the practical obstacles he faced. Holmes was finally forced to relent at 11:59 PM (Carreyrou, 2019) when Bissel pointed out that there was no way he could arrange federal inspections of the old facility at such short notice. (Theranos, being a biotech company, would need to pass post-move inspection to ascertain it handled biological and chemical waste appropriately.)

By February 2008, Bissel was out, and his subordinate Ed Ruiz joined him. Ruiz had disobeyed Holmes' order to dig through Bissel's emails in order to unearth some dirt on him (Carreyrou, 2019).

Initial User Tests

Meanwhile, Ana Arriola's old colleagues Justin Maxwell and Mike Bauerly found out indirectly that their boss had resigned. This sort of thing was common at Theranos where employees who irked Holmes didn't receive any sort of acknowledgment with regards to their departure. All that existed were rumors which were made worse thanks to Holmes' insane paranoia.

Joined by Aaron Moore (Carreyrou, 2019), the duo decided it was not an opportune moment to move companies, despite their misgivings. After all, the new offices were clearly a major upgrade and they reasoned, much like the rest of the valley, that Theranos was doing something right.

Tony Nugent was still struggling to get the Behar-designed case to work. However, time was ticking for the product design team and they decided to conduct a few user experience tests with the Edison. Their first impression of the system was not good. Even by the unpolished nature of first time products, the Edison looked like something a high schooler had put together for a project.

The robot's arms made a whiny noise when they moved and the apparatus constantly broke the pipettes. The cartridge itself was liable to break and thus, its overall reliability was poor, despite being a major upgrade over the 1.0. These user tests confirmed something Moore had long since suspected: The devices were far from easy to use.

In the previous studies that Holmes had carried out on the cancer patients in Tennessee, she had declared that the patients had adopted the 1.0 with ease and without any difficulty. Now, the 1.0 worked on different principles from the Edison but the method of transferring blood from the finger to cartridge was the same. Like everything else that came out of Holmes' mouth, this was a lie and the only person who could verify this, Edmond Ku, had long since been fired.

Here was what patients needed to do in order to transfer blood from their fingers to the cartridge. First, they needed to prick their fingers and coax some blood out of the tiny prick. Second, they needed to use the transfer pen to suck the drop of blood into the pen. Third, they needed to press a button on the pen which would push the blood into the cartridge's tubes. After doing all of this, there was the small matter of the amount of blood not being sufficient enough to deliver a result.

Therefore, another prick was required and the whole process had to be repeated again and again. At Theranos, it was common for people who tested the Edison to constantly prick their fingers, sometimes for hours on end, in order to coax a result. Of course, they didn't know whether the failure was a problem on the chemistry part or on the design part since only Holmes spoke to both teams.

This pattern was replicated during the user tests Moore and Bauerly carried out and they were extremely disappointed with the whole experience. Moore duly applied for a position with the sales team, not seeing much of a future with the product design side of things.

The Pharmaceutical Industry

Holmes had long been a one-woman sales team for Theranos. The initial studies and presentations to drug companies had been carried out by herself and an associate. The expansion of Theranos proved to be a problem for her since she could no longer keep glossing over the fact that, unbelievably, Theranos still didn't have an actual product.

Therefore, it was essential for her to recruit someone who would be unquestioningly loyal to her as the head of sales. Tim Kemp, in charge of Bioinformatics, was already on board and was more than willing to fabricate data in order to please prospective clients. A willing sales head would enable Holmes to buy more time to develop her product and keep the money rolling in at the same time.

The man she hired, Todd Surdey, was absolutely the opposite. A consummate sales executive, Surdey had a long and successful career with a variety of technology companies, most recently with SAP. In short, if there was even a semblance of a product, Surdey would be the guy to sell it. Holmes, however, had nothing of the sort.

Once he came on board, Surdey discovered that Holmes wasn't shy about making promises to prospective customers. A lot of the pharmaceutical companies would inquire whether the devices could be customized. Holmes always answered in the affirmative. This wasn't a red flag by itself but after a while, it was obvious that Theranos could do nothing of the sort, given that it was barely able to get the Edison to work.

Surdey then discovered something that got his alarm bells ringing. Always curious about the sorts of number Holmes kept throwing about, he tracked down one of the revenue spreadsheets, which were being prepared by the sales team instead of the still non-existent CFO, and dug into the numbers. He stumbled onto yet another instance of outright fraud Holmes was committing towards her investors.

The contracts that were signed with the drug companies promised numbers of the sort that Holmes had been quoting. However, there was a catch: Every company began its relationship with Theranos via a validation period. This was the period when sample tests would be conducted and results verified. Along with the results, the companies were then free to request customization and modifications to the product in order to proceed. The net revenue from the validation phase was a paltry $100,000, and the companies were free to walk if the validation period wasn't successful.

Thus, Holmes was constantly raising money on the basis of pie in the sky numbers which had almost no chance of materializing. Here, it's important to note that it wasn't the practice itself which alarmed Surdey (Carreyrou, 2019). It was the size of the numbers that made this untenable to him. Inflation of prospective revenue is a common practice amongst valley startups, after all. This phenomenon will be explored in detail in a later chapter.

Much like Avie Tevanian before him, Surdey's next move was to send these details to the man who was supposed to be in charge of the whole thing, but was instead asleep at the wheel – Don Lucas. Separately, he also brought the firm's in-house counsel, Michael Esquivel, on board with these findings.

Lucas wasn't completely asleep this time around, perhaps because Surdey was the son-in-law of BJ Cassin, a successful tech investor and member of Theranos' board. He convened a board meeting and during this, it was decided that Holmes would be replaced as CEO and someone more experienced would be appointed. Holmes would remain on the board and the idea was to help her learn the ropes, given her young age.

Holmes was summoned by the board and Lucas and the rest of them laid the case against her. Over the course of the next two hours, though, Holmes convinced the board, who were squarely against her, to give her another chance. According to Tom Brodeen, a board member and former CEO of various big companies, it was a masterful performance (Carreyrou, 2019) in an extremely tough situation, one in which seasoned CEOs would have found difficult.

However, Holmes managed to convince the board of her sincerity to change her management style and apologized for her actions which misled them thus far. She stayed on as CEO.

Billion Dollar Facade

A few weeks later, Esquivel and Surdey were gone. The loss of such good employees further convinced Justin Maxwell, Aaron Moore, and Mike Bauerly that Theranos was a madhouse. Maxwell, in what seems to be a comical move, recommended Holmes watch the TV show 'The Office' to learn about management. Moore was asked to quit by Nugent out of frustration and insulted by him on the way out for good measure. Baurely left in the December of 2008 (Carreyrou, 2019).

Holmes had survived a coup and had seen all the transplants from Apple come and go from Theranos. Roy, the sole voice of reason, had long since departed and all that was left were sycophants and a pathetically star struck board, completely incapable of doing the job it was supposed to.

Chapter 5: Further Trials And A Major Deal

By the middle of 2009, Theranos was chugging along, riding its way to constantly higher net worth, made even more absurd by the fact that the company didn't even have a single working product. Ideas have always attracted funding in Silicon Valley but never had an idea attracted this amount of it.

Holmes was firmly in charge of her company. By this point, she had maneuvered the board into giving her 99% of the voting rights and Don Lucas remained a pale figurehead of a chairman, having neglected to do the job he was supposed to. Still, the investors had no clue what was happening within the company thanks to Holmes' secretive and draconian workplace rules.

Given the high level departures and constant turnover, which was now a worry for a company of Theranos' size, a new management strategy was in order. Holmes promptly doubled down on the existing strategy by hiring a curious character to senior management by the name of Ramesh Balwani.

Always Sunny At Theranos

Ramesh Balwani, who went by the moniker "Sunny" for some reason, was born in Pakistan. He arrived in America in 1986 to pursue a degree in computer science and went on to have a successful career at Lotus and later, Microsoft. In 1999, at the height of the dot-com market boom, he became a minority partner at a startup by the name of commercebid.com.

B2B e-commerce was receiving breathless valuations in the stock market and CommerceBid was right in the thick of the B2B sector. The entire company was based around the idea of designing a live auction site which would enable companies to receive better bids from its suppliers.

A larger company in this niche, Commerce One, had recently gone public and seen its stock zoom 1000% over a year. In the market with a lot of cash, thanks to public money, Commerce One was on the hunt. CommerBid's live auction system seemed appealing and shortly, an offer for $232 million followed. Balwani, as a junior partner, cleared over $40 million in the deal.

This certified his vision of himself as a genius businessman and did nothing to reduce the size of his ego. Five months later, Commerce One went bankrupt but clearly his riches were a result of extraordinary business acumen, not mere luck. A few years later, Balwani decided to travel to China on a study exchange group and it was there he met Holmes.

Balwani and Holmes struck a chord, despite the massive age gap between the two. Holmes saw a kindred spirit in Balwani and eventually, the two began a relationship which was known to Holmes' parents and close friends. People would remark at the strange dynamic the two had, with Balwani exhorting her to make more money and Holmes rarely showing much affection or even acknowledging him publicly (Carreyrou, 2019).

Either way, around mid 2009, Holmes was perhaps feeling the

pressure at Theranos and brought Balwani on board as a director and de facto equal.

Hiring Strategy

One of Balwani's first tasks appears to have been to try and find a modicum of stability with regards to the company's hiring strategy. While constant turnover at a smaller size could be managed for a company with the pedigree of Theranos, at its current size, it simply wasn't feasible.

Given the draconian management style prevalent, clearly an employee with options was not a good fit. After all, as Holmes' misadventures with ex-Apple employees had shown, an employee could always leave on their own volition if allowed to. Balwani thus reasoned that the best way to maintain management control, as well as limit turnover, was to use the H1-B visa program.

The H-1B visa allows non-citizens to live and work in the United States legally. It has a total term of six years during which most immigrant workers apply for a Green Card, which is permanent residency. An H1 employee is severely curtailed in terms of options. While the rules are different now, back in 2009, if an employee was fired from their job, they had an extremely limited period, usually days, within which they had to secure a new job.

This naturally made a lot of H1 workers potential white collar slaves to an unscrupulous boss. With the majority of such workers coming from India and China in order to support families back home, the possibility of such employees quitting or even talking back to a boss was, and is, remote.

Data from US immigration shows a steady rise in the number of H1 visa applications and subsequent green card applications sponsored by Theranos starting from 2009 onwards. ("THERANOS INC. - Historical applications for H-1B visa and green card sponsorship applications", 2019) Mind you, these weren't low level employees Theranos was hiring. The majority of these applications were for Ph.D. graduates to work in the labs which Theranos would eventually set up to test patient samples.

While employees felt Holmes was draconian, Balwani was viewed as an out and out monster. Accounts of his behavior from ex-employees at Theranos bear this fact. Curiously, almost none of them on the record of testimonies come from former H-1B employees. After all, if you're going to need a job in order to continue living in the States, it hardly pays to tell on your former boss, even if he was an unhinged psychopath.

The nameless and faceless H1 employees were perhaps the biggest victims of the fraud that Holmes carried out. While the few patients Theranos defrauded received settlements, it is unlikely any of these employees ever received any form of restitution, given the state of H-1B laws and the lack of practical rights such employees have.

Medical Trials

Around the same time Balwani came on board and began terrorizing everyone, Holmes managed to recruit an old friend of hers from Stanford by the name of Chelsea Burkett. Burkett was, at the time, working at another valley startup and was looking for a change. Given what she knew about Holmes and the general buzz around Theranos within the valley, she accepted.

Burkett joined the client solutions group which was where Theranos representatives reached out to drug companies to convince them to let Theranos run validation studies. The idea was that if the validation period passed, the company would commit to further business. It was for this further business upon which Holmes was basing her entire valuation for the business, as we saw previously.

The first surprise Burkett received was the news of Balwani working alongside Holmes. She had known of their relationship but did not know they were working together, which didn't seem like a good idea, especially since she guessed the personal relationship hadn't been disclosed to investors or to any of the employees. Interestingly, Holmes informed Nugent that they were not romantically involved when he questioned her (Carreyrou, 2019).

Burkett was never a fan of Balwani and her dislike for him only intensified when she discovered the malfunctioning Edisons. Balwani was well aware of the malfunctions and constantly blamed the "wireless connection", no matter where they were. She soon caught a break from Balwani via a Centocor assignment. Centocor was a division of Johnson and Johnson and Theranos was to deploy the Edison to measure how patients were responding to asthma medication. The test was conducted by measuring the levels of IgE or immunoglobulin E in their blood. Accompanying Burkett on this trip was Daniel Young, an MIT graduate with a Ph.D. in bioengineering (Carreyrou, 2019).

Young's job was to add the skill of mathematical modeling to the test results Theranos would be receiving. The idea behind this was to enable Theranos to predict the reaction patients would have to the drugs that were being administered. The program Theranos would run for the purpose would rely on what now sounds like earlier versions of AI. The more data it was fed, the better it would 'learn' and the better predictive power it would have.

Of course, the catch in all this was that there was no data to be had from the Edisons. Whether due to Balwani's 'wireless' issues or due to some other legitimate reason, the devices were extremely finicky and quite often, Burkett had trouble getting results even when nothing was wrong. Over and above this, there was also the fact that the blood sample was usually too small for any meaningful result.

We will catch up with Young down the road where he would shed all semblance of his modeling role and fully embrace his true role as the token brainy guy who would help Holmes justify her web of lies when she was finally exposed. For now, he was an appendage of sorts to Burkett who was struggling to coax any results out of the Edisons.

Unbeknownst to her, Pfizer had notified Theranos of its unwillingness to continue forward after the cancer patient trials in Tennessee. In a letter to the company, Pfizer noted the vast discrepancies in the results and the large number of failures which made it unrealistic to continue. Holmes, for her part, retaliated with a twenty-six page letter (Carreyrou, 2019) which copped to the unreliability but provided little else in terms of justification or explanation for the results.

If anything, she drew attention to the fact that the patients themselves had placed the devices in less than ideal situations, thus implying that Theranos was not fully at fault. Either way, Pfizer discontinued its relationship with the company. No one except Balwani and Holmes knew about this, thanks to the information embargo they had imposed.

Burkett, meanwhile, flew to Antwerp, Belgium to conduct the trials and record data, or whatever there was of it. It was there that she discovered the range of issues which the Edison was susceptible to.

For starters, the wireless connection was an issue but this had nothing to do with the device itself, only with the transmission of results back to a server in Belgium. The real issues were with the design of the devices themselves. You might recall that the Edison was designed to perform a type of test called the Chemiluminescent Immunoassays, which relied on measuring the output of light in order to detect symptoms.

The problem was that the volume of liquid needed for the Edison to work resulted in over-dilution of the blood samples, which had to be small in accordance with the marketing material. Thus, there simply wasn't enough light being emitted for the device to measure since all of it was being absorbed by the over-diluted mixture.

Furthermore, for the device to actually work, it had to be maintained at a steady temperature of 34 degrees Celsius. When a test was being run, the device had two heaters inside it to maintain its temperature. However, in cooler or warmer settings, these were completely useless, thus resulting in the blood sample congealing or simply not flowing enough.

Thoroughly discouraged, Burkett returned to Palo Alto only to find that Holmes had moved on to another opportunity.

Swine Flu

Mexico at the time was caught in the throes of a swine flu epidemic and Holmes saw an opportunity to use the Edison to pitch another pie in the sky concept she had no hope of delivering on, but sounded smart enough for people to give her a chance to do it anyway.

Seth Michelson, the chief scientific officer, told Holmes of a mathematical model called Susceptible, Exposed, Infected, Resolved or SEIR for short, which could be used to predict where the epidemic would spread next. To do this, Theranos would need data and lots of it.

The next thing she knew, Burkett was on a plane to Mexico to spend months on end in a hospital, feeding samples from infected patients into the malfunctioning Edison. She wondered how Holmes was able to get the Mexican government to agree to this while there. Holmes had leveraged an old Stanford connection she had with a wealthy Mexican student whose family was close to the government.

Much to her chagrin, Burkett was accompanied by Balwani despite him not speaking a lick of Spanish nor having a medical background of any kind. He was simply there to yell and make sure Burkett didn't accidentally let slip to the government that the devices weren't working.

Worst of all, Burkett learned from scientists within Theranos, that performing a blood test to detect swine flu is a bit like examining your stomach to diagnose why your foot is hurting. The tests that detect swine flu rely on samples conducted via a nasal swab. When she brought this up with Holmes, the latter brushed it aside and told Burkett not to listen to those scientists – scientists Holmes had herself hired to work for Theranos.

Balwani, meanwhile, flew to Thailand where the epidemic had spread, and set up another study in extremely shady circumstances. There were allegations of bribery but nothing was proved. A colleague of Burkett's who flew in with Balwani to Thailand promptly quit upon returning.

The final straw for Burkett came when the aforementioned Mexican connection brought his father into Theranos' Palo Alto offices to have him tested for cancer symptoms or bio-markers. This appalled Burkett, and given the considerable number of red flags and disappearing colleagues (employees often joked of Balwani disappearing their colleagues after firing them) (Carreyrou, 2019), she approached Holmes and notified her of her decision to quit.

Holmes and Balwani encouraged her to leave immediately and quietly, without farewells of any kind. Thus, Burkett joined the ranks of the disappeared.

Commercial Attention

Dr. Jay Rosen had a problem. As part of the medical innovations team at Walgreens, the pharmacy chain that is not CVS, he was tasked with finding the next big idea which would propel the company into the future, whatever that meant. With America deeply mired in an economic crisis, innovation was far from people's minds at the time.

However, Rosen couldn't help but notice, like a lot of other Americans did, that the West Coast business scene was playing out very differently from those in the rest of the country. Silicon Valley seemed to be playing by a different set of rules. Around mid 2009 to early 2010, Facebook saw its private valuation rise to an eye watering $30 billion, and right in its wake were companies like Twitter.

Google had long since proved itself immune to economic cycles, having firmly established itself as not just a tech giant, but as a verb in the English language. Soon, Google would invest a considerable sum of money into a startup called Uber Cabs, which would go on to epitomize both the vision as well as the twisted nature of what the valley considered "business".

Walgreens, like other main street firms, was having a hard time competing in those economic times. It seemed natural that with tech seemingly disrupting everything in sight, (the iPhone had just consigned the telephone to history's trash can) the future of main street lay in the hands of valley tech and innovation.

Right on cue, he learned of an email Walgreens had received from someone named Elizabeth Holmes representing a valley startup named Theranos. The message she implied was simple: She was changing the future of health. Was Walgreens going to be a part of it?

In-Store Blood Tests

By early February 2010, Holmes and Balwani made their way out to Philadelphia, which is where Rosen worked, and presented information which made his head spin. Theranos had the ability, via its patented, futuristic Edison device, to conduct 192 blood tests (Carreyrou, 2019) with just a single prick of the patient's finger.

Rosen also received the new spiel Holmes was putting on these days, about her being terrified of needles and equating people's fear of needles and blood tests to being afraid of snakes or spiders. Like everyone else before him, Rosen was taken in by Holmes' story and Walgreens decided to pounce on the opportunity, post haste.

To help them out with the deal, Walgreens hired a man named Kevin Hunter who ran a medical consulting business named Colaborate. Hunter had previously worked for eight years at Quest Labs, a firm that was established in the areas Theranos was targeting, and after receiving his M.B.A, set up Colaborate to advise private equity and hedge fund clients about medical lab issues and processes. In short, he knew his field better than most.

By mid-summer 2010, a batch of Walgreens executives, including the CFO Wade Miquelon, had flown to Palo Alto to meet with Theranos. The plan was to have a two day session where the executives would hash out the details of the plan to move forward and Hunter would have the opportunity to advise as well as inspect the labs – something he was very keen on.

Holmes had marketed Theranos as having a fully operational commercial lab which was equipped to conduct all 192 tests on the list. The reality was far more sobering. Theranos had a basic R&D lab, and since the Edison was built to conduct Chemiluminescent Immunoassays, out of the 192 tests, only a very small number could actually be conducted.

The first thing the executives noticed was a Lamborghini parked right in front of the building despite there not being a parking spot there. This was Balwani's idea of impressing people with his wealth and he generally fit the stereotype of a person who would do these sorts of things.

He seemed to wear expensive clothes, expensive labels at least, but still managed to look unkempt. He wore jewelry and fancy watches but looked like someone who had just robbed a bank (Carreyrou, 2019). Either way, Holmes occupied the client-facing role with Balwani as the backup, so presumably the executives weren't put off by all of this.

Accompanying the executives, Hunter noticed the extreme lengths to which Theranos went in the name of privacy and trade secrets. The executive were shepherded down a path into a room which was screened off completely. At one point, Hunter requested to go to the restroom and Holmes and Balwani responded by saying that security was paramount and that he would have to be escorted (Carreyrou, 2019).

Balwani accompanied him and upon being asked where the lab was, he responded that it was downstairs. Holmes brushed aside Hunter's request to be shown the lab, something which was standard practice from a due diligence standpoint before concluding a deal. However, the due diligence part of things seemed moot since the Walgreens executives, led by Rosen, seemed star struck by Holmes.

They duly inked a deal for a pilot project whereby the Edison would be placed in up to ninety stores nationwide by Spring of 2011. In addition, the company would purchase $50 million worth of cartridges and would lend Theranos an additional $25 million. Hunter was a bit alarmed by the speed with which Walgreens, his client, was moving.

As they rose up for lunch, Hunter once again requested to view the lab. Holmes motioned for Rosen to come with her outside at this point. Upon his return, Rosen told Hunter that a lab visit was out of the question, let alone a live Vitamin D test that was next on Hunter's request list.

At a loss to understand why Walgreens even wanted his help at this point, Hunter then received a full dose of Holmes' paranoia. The executives were made to leave in shifts in order to arrive at the chosen restaurant at staggered intervals. Once there, they were escorted to a private room where Holmes was already waiting. Hunter, not unreasonably, thought he had entered the twilight zone. If the intention was to not draw any attention, then what should be made of Balwani's garish Lamborghini in the parking lot?

By this time, Hunter had enough time to observe the personalities of the two Theranos executives. Holmes, it struck him, was going to great lengths to emulate Steve Jobs. There was the black turtleneck and slacks along with the obviously affected deep voice. Then there was the kale shake she constantly sipped and talks of disruption. Beneath the veneer though, Hunter realized Holmes' knowledge of even the most rudimentary blood tests was lacking. Then there were the excuses. Hunter had informed Theranos over two weeks ago that he intended to conduct a Vitamin D test using Rosen's blood and have it verified with the results from the nearby Stanford Hospital.

Holmes had brushed this aside by saying that Theranos had not been given enough notice. Meanwhile, Balwani, as was his wont, was making an impression that was diametrically opposite to his intention. He was arrogant and acted superior to everything around him. Walgreens' suggestion that their IT department be brought on elicited a scoff from Balwani and no real further discussion (Carreyrou, 2019).

Having said that, Hunter also noticed that he was the only one in the room who wasn't buying what was going on. Rosen was a giddy schoolgirl and the rest of the executives followed his lead. Holmes did seem to have a magnetic personality, which, in spite of Balwani's presence, attracted people, especially older men, to her like flies.

This seems a controversial statement but as the reader will later see, every single one of Holmes' most ardent backers and supporters, even when she was unmasked as a fraud, fit a pattern, both in personality as well as background.

A Study In Excuses

On the second day of the visit, Miquelon signed a deal with Theranos and for his troubles was gifted an American flag. Hunter was left wondering why he had even been contacted by Walgreens in the first place as they made their way back to the East coast.

In the September of that year, Walgreens threw a special party to announce the collaboration and Holmes and Balwani, along with a handful of Edisons, made the trip. As a special gesture, the Walgreens executives were encouraged to get their blood tested and all of them lined up to have their fingers pricked. Although he wasn't present, Hunter finally saw his chance to see the results the devices produced.

He had, by this time, filed a report with Walgreens which warned that Theranos might be exaggerating the ability of its machines and that no proof had been provided at this point. He also recommended that one of his colleagues be embedded within Theranos in order to ensure the pilot project was implemented smoothly. Nothing came of this report.

During the by now routine, weekly conference call, Hunter asked Holmes about the results of the blood tests, to which Holmes responded that she could not release them to him since he wasn't a doctor. However, Rosen was one, and she conceded that Balwani would follow up with him regarding this. However, months passed and there was no word of the tests. Much like the by now neutered Don Lucas, Rosen was firmly asleep at the wheel.

The test results then took a firm backseat to what Hunter saw as an act of extreme irresponsibility and one which was legally questionable. A little bit of background information is required for this. Medical tests in the United States are regulated by a combination of two bodies: CMS and FDA. The CMS (Centre for Medicare and Medicaid Services) supervises labs via a law termed CLIA which stands for Clinical Laboratory Improvement Amendments, which was enacted in 1988 (Carreyrou, 2019).

The FDA (Food and Drug Administration) regulates the equipment used for testing within laboratories. In order for a lab to pass muster, it needs approval from both bodies. However, there was a gray area in the law. Tests which were simple and home-based, such as using a thermometer, were termed "CLIA waived" and these didn't need any prior approval from either body.

Now, there was a gray area in the law when it came to laboratories, which is best illustrated via an example. Let's say a blood centrifuge machine, which is used to prepare blood samples for furthers tests, needs to be certified. The CMS would inspect the lab technicians' accreditation and general facilities. The FDA would inspect the machine itself and would certify it for its intended use.

If the lab, however, started using this centrifuge machine to measure someone's temperature (obviously unrealistic but this is just an example), this is a gray area. The authorities rely on the technicians' and lab operators' ethics in order to ensure tests are conducted properly and that the equipment is being used correctly. It is in this gray area that Holmes decided to slot in the Edison.

Technically, since the Edison was a completely new device, what was its intended use? Holmes initially earmarked the Edison to conduct CLIA waived tests; therefore FDA approval was not required for the machines. However, midway through the Walgreens courting phase, she indicated that the tests Theranos would perform were "laboratory developed", which firmly fell into the gray area previously described.

This is a pretty common valley tactic where regulation is usually viewed as an obstacle as opposed to existing for a reason. The difference here is that Holmes was playing fast and loose with medical tests, which would have immediate consequences not unlike taxi regulations or private data.

Hunter considered this switch a major red flag and promptly suggested conducting a fifty-patient study at Stanford Hospital to validate the Edisons. He was denied this request. Next, he asked for some sort of report or study which validated the instruments and the technology within.

Theranos had always cited two sources which validated this: One was the claim that ten of the largest pharmaceutical companies had certified its technology through clinical trials. We've already seen what actually took place during those trials. The second source was a review which had been commissioned by Rosen from Johns Hopkins.

Hunter was unable to get anyone from a pharmaceutical company to validate Theranos' claims. As a last resort, he got his hands on the Hopkins Review which turned out to be a two-page document, or a two-page joke as he saw it. It listed details of a meeting Holmes and Rosen had with Hopkins representatives in which she walked them through its technology.

Hopkins noted that the technology seemed sound but clarified that they had not verified anything independently. Attached to this was a disclaimer that the review did not amount to an endorsement of Theranos by Hopkins. Surely, in light of all this, Hunter felt, Walgreens would see the light?

Rosen brushed his concerns aside, and an executive, Trish Lipinski, informed Hunter that Holmes no longer welcomed his presence at their meetings. Thus, despite being hired to conduct due diligence, Walgreens sidelined the one person who was actually doing his job.

Aside from Rosen being smitten by Holmes, the reason Walgreens aggressively pursued the Theranos deal was due to its inferiority complex when it came to their market position as compared to CVS. Tired of always being second best in a two man fight, Walgreens desperately clung to Theranos as its savior. Thus, Holmes always had the upper hand in every negotiation and even implying that she was ready to walk was enough to send the executives scampering.

Walgreens would soon pay the price for their actions. While all this was going on, Holmes had managed to snag another victim.

Safeway

Steve Burd was a CEO on the wane when Holmes got in touch with him. Burd was one of the most respected CEOs in America, having turned Safeway stores from a failing business to a thriving supermarket chain. Along the way, he helped pioneer innovative healthcare programs for his employees and earned their respect and loyalty.

However, as of late, Safeway was having issues. The rise of online stores had caught Burd flat-footed, and while addressing these concerns, he realized that the costs of the in-house medical program would bankrupt the company someday. Not wanting to cut benefits, he needed an innovative approach that would guarantee the same level of benefits at much lower costs.

Enter Holmes and her dud machines. Burd, like Rosen, was smitten by her, gifting her white orchids and toy private jets (Carreyrou,

2019). Soon, Safeway inked deals which made it the exclusive provider of Theranos blood tests in supermarkets. The move would cost Burd his job eventually.

Thus, by the end of 2010 and early 2011, Theranos signed its first commercial deals. Holmes had claimed a number of deals prior to this but it's a sobering thought that it was only now that she had managed to sign honest-to-God customers. Having done this, she realized that she had created a huge problem for herself.

The solution was to continue doing what she is best at: Lie, intimidate and charm.

Chapter 6: Bigger Victims

The deals with Safeway and Walgreens were signed with the intention of beginning immediately. Burd, the CEO of Safeway, soon ordered a remodeling of all stores to accommodate wellness centers. These centers, designed to look luxurious on Holmes' insistence, would be where customers could walk up and have their blood tested. The results would be available far sooner than traditional labs.

This delivery promise is something else Holmes added to her pitch at some point. From an initial vision of a wearable patch which would regulate medication, Holmes had arrived at a vision of clinics whereby patients would only need to provide a speck of blood and receive almost instantaneous results. It didn't matter that she could deliver none of these things.

However, her vision kept getting bigger and bigger despite Theranos still not having even a single working product, be it a patch, a prototype, or even the Edison. Having promised the world to everyone, she decided it was time to build another product.

She christened it the "miniLab."

Business As Usual

The reason Theranos needed a new product is that the Edison was limited in the number of tests it could actually perform.

Immunoassays rely on the presence of antibodies to deliver a result, and this was all the Edison could do. Furthermore, it did it poorly. A key feature of Holmes' management is her failure to distinguish between a prototype and a finished product.

While most companies treated a prototype as the beginning, thanks to her lies piling up around her, Holmes was forced to treat it as the finished product. Thus, as she kept promising things which were real only in her head, the teams designing the product struggled to keep pace with her claims.

Not that any of them knew about it. Holmes' paranoia hadn't abated and the embargo on information was still strictly in place. Employees only knew that commercial deals were inked but they knew little else. They were repeatedly told by Balwani and Holmes that the company was making great strides and asking for proof of these strides usually resulted in a firing.

Tyrant

While Holmes was primarily outwardly focused, the task of in-house management fell to Balwani. His managerial style reflected his subcontinental roots, with him adhering to a master/slave relationship when it came to his employees. He expected everyone to dedicate their entire lives to Theranos and even went so far as to monitor employees' clock in and out times (Carreyrou, 2019).

Video surveillance of those he disliked was routine and he monitored employee emails constantly in order to find some excuse to yell at someone. By this point, his strategy of hiring mostly H-1B employees was in full swing, and as a result, Theranos got itself a bunch of employees who were fully dependant on their employer without any sort of practical recourse.

Those who did have options to leave usually did and it's unclear why those who stayed on did. Holmes at some point hired her younger brother, Christian, to work at Theranos. He wasn't very clear about his role at the company at first, and was reported to have sat at his desk reading ESPN all day (Carreyrou, 2019).

Christian shortly hired his fraternity brothers out of Duke University and the group came to be known as the "frat pack" within the company (Carreyrou, 2019). They were in charge of communications officially, but played a variety of roles as required. Despite their lofty connections, they weren't completely immune to Balwani's ego.

Taking breaks was strongly discouraged at Theranos and to pass the time, one of the frat packs took to scheduling gym visits for the entire group while avoiding Balwani's gaze. They would schedule staggered exits and re-entries so as to avoid suspicion (Carreyrou, 2019). The frat pack, right from the start, had full access to the strategy meetings involving Walgreens and Safeway, despite long-time employees being shut out.

Meanwhile, Steve Jobs passed away and the event was marked at Theranos by flying the Apple flag at half-mast. Employees noticed an increase in the intensity which Holmes mimicked Jobs after this event. Jobs' biography, written by Walter Isaacson, was released and allegedly, employees were able to determine at which page she was reading depending on her behavior (Carreyrou, 2019).

Holmes even went as far as christening the miniLab the "4S", after the iPhone version that was released a day after Jobs passed away. Meanwhile, given the mountain of unrealistic stuff she and Balwani were promising their clients, Holmes began pressuring the engineering team in charge of developing the miniLab.

Billion Dollar Facade

If the regular workforce was under pressure, the engineering team was under extra special scrutiny. Holmes expected her employees to lay their lives down for the company but in typical Holmesian style – she never communicated the reason for the urgency or the existence of a deadline.

She and Balwani often strolled the hallways together, talking in whispers and Balwani would sometimes even accompany her into the restroom. This led to employees joking that the two of them were perhaps snorting cocaine in there (Carreyrou, 2019). Employees fell in and out of favor with the duo for strange reasons. One employee was given the cold shoulder because his sister declined a job with Theranos.

Another was put on a leave of absence because he worked on a personal engineering project on the weekends, weekends he should have been spending at Theranos, according to Holmes. At the annual Christmas party, Holmes addressed her staff and made it very clear that she viewed the 4S as being the most important thing humanity would ever build (Carreyrou, 2019). Anyone who disagreed should leave immediately.

This messianic attitude Holmes carried about her was evident to everyone who met her and the bigger her lies became, the greater was this attitude. She and Balwani routinely tried pitting co-workers against each other, especially those whom they knew were close. Employees who resigned were completely ignored by the duo during their notice periods.

On one such occasion, they forgot to conduct an exit interview with an employee, and upon finding out that the employee had left without signing a confidentiality agreement, they sent the police after him, despite having no case. Their complaint was that the employee had stolen, in Balwani's words, "property in his mind" (Carreyrou,

2019).

Burd Asleep

Meanwhile, at Safeway, things were getting delayed. Steve Burd, the CEO, was constantly being pressed about the less than stellar results his company was posting. In desperation, on an analyst's call, he disclosed a "wellness play" that Safeway was heavily investing in. This would turn the company's fortunes around.

The fact that Safeway was not a drugstore or even in the medical field didn't seem to matter. Also, this being the first time Burd had disclosed anything of this nature, the financial media began to pick this up. All of this only increased the pressure on Burd and his team to deliver.

None of this pressure translated into Holmes delivering, though. Much like the long succession of older, more powerful men she had hoodwinked up to this point, Burd was star struck by Holmes. The team in charge of implementing the new concept within Safeway did not have access to Holmes; only Burd did. This was instigated by Holmes after her bad experience with Hunter at Walgreens. Safeway was shelling out $350 million to remodel its stores but Burd still saw it fit to keep Holmes isolated and protected.

Holmes, meanwhile, was busy inventing new excuses to explain delays. The Kobe earthquake that struck Japan in early 2011 was responsible for delays in cartridge production, she claimed at one point, and everyone except Burd saw right through it. Being the man in charge though, it was Burd's opinion that counted.

Safeway guarded the details of the wellness play with its life. Even store managers in the pilot locations had no idea what it was all about, beyond the remodeling that took place. Finally, in early 2012, after at least a year's worth of delays, Theranos was ready. Ready to run a pilot project at one location: Safeway's corporate campus in Pleasanton, CA.

We now know that the reason for these delays was the fact that Theranos hadn't developed the 4S to any respectable stage, but at the time, no such information was available, of course. Safeway reasoned that something was better than nothing and went ahead with the plan full steam, convinced that Theranos would soon occupy its intended place within their stores.

The facility within the campus had a small lab, five examination rooms and was staffed by a doctor and three nurses (Carreyrou, 2019). The check-ups were free and employees were incentivized to use the facility. Signs around the facility proclaimed "Testing done by Theranos" (Carreyrou, 2019).

The employee clinic was overseen by Safeway's chief medical officer, Kent Bradley. A US Army veteran, Bradley was soft spoken and extremely curious about Theranos' devices. He was first surprised when he learned that Theranos would not actually be placing any devices within the facility.

The second surprising aspect of the whole thing was that the technicians in the clinic collected blood twice. Once with a pinprick, and the second time via a hypodermic needle, called a "venipuncture". In other words, they were doing it the old fashioned way along with the pinprick which Theranos had lobbied.

Bradley wondered, reasonably, as to why the venipuncture was required if the devices required just a small drop of blood? Then there was the time it took to receive results. Bradley's understanding was that the results would be almost instantaneous. Given that there were no devices present, this was a pipe dream. However, many patients ended up waiting for as long as two weeks.

Upon examining the reports, Bradley was further surprised to see that Theranos was outsourcing a lot of the tests to a lab named ARUP, which was a big, well-established laboratory in San Francisco (Carreyrou, 2019), and conducting only a small number of tests itself.

As a final surprise, Bradley discovered that the results were all wrong. Perfectly healthy patients were given results that indicated near death. Bradley swiftly instructed his patients to get themselves tested with either Quest or LabCorp, which were long established and trusted companies. When the results from the retests showed nothing wrong, Bradley was alarmed (Carreyrou, 2019).

Digging deeper into the data, he discovered that only the results of tests which were conducted by Theranos were faulty. The ones from ARUP were perfectly fine. Deeply disturbed, he escalated the situation, all the way to Burd. Burd brushed aside the data in front of him and chose to trust Holmes' assertion that Theranos' technology was sound and worked perfectly.

We already know that Burd was beyond negligent by this point in time. However, given the state of the miniLab, how exactly was Holmes managing to produce test results?

East Meadow Circle

With the miniLabs nowhere near complete, the Edisons incapable of giving reliable results for the few tests it could conduct and the 1.0 long since consigned to the trash can, Holmes turned to the only solution that was left open to her in order to produce results.

Around April 2012, Theranos leased a small building at East Meadow Circle in Palo Alto. The money that was now pouring in from the commercial contracts as well as other investors, who will be looked at shortly, enabled Theranos to complete a second move. This time, the company moved to a larger building on Hillview which was a former home of Facebook – another company that was producing nothing but was somehow one of the most valuable corporations on Earth.

The lab work was now conducted on separate premises from the bigger Hillview headquarters. This new lab was in compliance with CLIA and was thus federally regulated. However, readers will recall from the Walgreens episode that Holmes was operating in a regulatory gray area here.

The CLIA licenses, which were issued by the CMS, were pretty easy to obtain. The CMS outsourced the inspection work to state agencies and it so happened that at the time, the local agency was severely understaffed and underfunded. As a result, it is doubtful whether routine inspections were conducted or not. Theranos was therefore able to skirt by a lot of regulatory requirements.

What's more, the lab didn't contain a single Theranos device. With the miniLabs still under development at the R&D labs at the headquarters, Holmes stocked the new space with commercially available blood and body fluid analyzers. Siemens, DiaSorin, and Abbott Labs machines populated the center and were used to carry out tests.

One would have expected these machines to guarantee correct results. However, thanks to the hiring practices and policies of Theranos, the majority of technicians who staffed the place were severely untrained or simply not qualified. Thus, the samples which were taken from Safeway employees in Pleasanton arrived by courier to the East Meadow lab to be analyzed by incompetent technicians in off-the-shelf analyzers.

Accounts of the shenanigans at the East Meadow lab were available thanks to Diana Dupuy who was a clinical laboratory scientist (CLS) and had trained at the prestigious MD Anderson Cancer Institute. She remains the only person who has provided accounts of how Theranos tested samples without remaining anonymous (Carreyrou, 2019).

Dupuy spent seven years training to become a CLS and thus had full exposure to CLIA requirements. According to her, a number of her fellow technicians at the lab lacked proper training. The list of blunders she observed are too numerous to list but among them were: Improper handling of reagents, running tests on miscalibrated equipment, following wrong QA procedures on analyzers, performing tasks that the person was not trained to do, and so on.

With every transgression, she duly documented and reprimanded her errant colleagues. However, she hadn't contented with the boss she had, who was none other than Balwani. With every email he received from Dupuy, Balwani grew increasingly agitated and it was only a matter of time before Dupuy would be fired. As it was, she soldiered on, thinking she was doing her job.

This mishandling of patient samples explains why Theranos was generating wrong results despite using machines perfectly capable of producing correct ones. The quality of the CLS is just as important as that of the equipment. Balwani had no interest or understanding of this point. Furthermore, the technicians who were drawing blood at the Safeway premises were not trained properly and Dupuy often received samples which were useless for testing.

What Theranos did with the pinprick samples is not known. All of the above only deals with the venipuncture samples. Dupuy was shortly sent on a training exercise in order to master a new Siemens analyzer Theranos had produced, and on her return, she found herself face-to-face with the Lord Commander of lab testing – Balwani, himself.

Dupuy noticed the lab was spotless and found herself in a meeting room with Balwani telling her that he had failed to spot any of the issues she had mentioned to him. Furthermore, by letting her boyfriend into the building to help her with her luggage for the previous trip, she was in breach of security regulations and was therefore fired.

Then, in a seemingly magnanimous act, he called Dupuy's supervisor over and asked him whether she was required. Upon receiving a positive answer, Balwani played the benevolent God and let Dupuy off with a warning.

A few weeks later, Dupuy sent an email noting that one of the lab's suppliers had halted deliveries because of unpaid bills. This time, she was escorted out of the building by security without a chance to even gather her personal belongings. Upon sending an angry email to Balwani and Holmes about the matter, she was allowed to gather them and promptly began receiving threatening emails from the company's outside counsel.

The law firm, Wilson Sonsini, was one of Silicon Valley's most powerful, and their emails warned her of dire consequences of breaking her confidentiality agreements and sharing any company related material. Dupuy, initially, thought of fighting the case but in the face of unrelenting pressure and strong arm tactics, relented and gave in.

This is a pattern that Holmes employed against everyone who opposed her. Those she could not legally threaten, like Hunter, she isolated. Those who she could, like Dupuy, she bullied and battered into submission.

Burd Out

On January 2nd 2013, Safeway put out a press release informing everyone that their current CEO Steve Burd would be retiring in May. It was a thinly veiled firing by a board that was fed up with non-existent progress on the company's flagship wellness scheme. Moreover, the common sentiment was that Burd had lost sight of the fact that Safeway's primary business was to sell groceries, not deploy wellness spas.

The previous year, Burd had gone around assuring everyone of the fact that the wellness centers in stores would soon be operational. When executives came up with alternative use for the space, their ideas were shot down because, according to Burd, Holmes did not want to give up on the space.

Say what you will of Holmes; she somehow managed to hoodwink an experienced CEO into renting her space at zero cost to her despite producing no results for over three years. This performance deserves an award of some sort. Anyway, Burd was far too gone to see the situation for what it was.

Even as he was leaving his post, Burd reiterated how Theranos and Holmes would change the world. Once he retired, after the appropriate length of gardening time, Burd set up his very own startup consulting firm, Burd Health, with a view to advise companies on how to reduce their employee healthcare costs. Given his proximity to Theranos, he figured Holmes would love to collaborate on ideas.

There was just one problem: Holmes had no use for him anymore and never returned his calls (Carreyrou, 2019).

Civilians No More

No one can explain the logic behind a lot of Holmes' behavior. After signing two huge commercial contracts, the first ones she had successfully managed to close, it would have been common sense to knuckle down and actually produce some semblance of a working product.

Instead, she kept hunting bigger and bigger game. These actions of hers bear out the earlier observation about her having no interest in changing the world or whatever else she thought she was trying to achieve. All she cared about was fame and money. In August 2011, right around the time when Walgreens and Safeway were lured, Holmes managed to trap the biggest fish of them all.

At a social get together at the Marines Memorial Club in San Francisco, Holmes somehow managed to pitch the idea of deploying Theranos' blood analyzers in active war zones to General James Mattis, nicknamed "Mad Dog", who was head of U.S central command. Caught in a decade long war in Afghanistan, Mattis was convinced that this device would be a game changer for his troops.

Holmes' idea was to have the devices deployed with soldiers on the ground and with just a pinprick of blood, diagnose and treat wounded soldiers faster, with greater accuracy. Mattis loved the idea and ordered his subordinates to set up a live field test ASAP. To get there though, Holmes would first have to tackle regulatory hurdles.

Disapproval

Later that year, Holmes found herself hosting a small military delegation at the Palo Alto headquarters trying to explain her plan to have the Edison devices deployed in the field. Among those present was the deputy director for the division of regulated activities and compliance, out of Fort Derrick, Maryland: LTC David Shoemaker (Carreyrou, 2019). Shoemaker had a Ph.D. in microbiology and years of research in vaccines for dangerous diseases, some of which had been weaponized during times of warfare.

He was also the Army's foremost expert on FDA regulations, having completed a one year fellowship on the subject recently. Having heard of the regulatory umbrella under which Holmes was trying to deploy her devices - the previously described gray area - Shoemaker let her know that this approach would simply not fly.

The FDA was well aware of this gray area and considered it impractical to regulate each and every tiny lab to operate out of it, instead relying on state authorities and the lab managers themselves to hold themselves to a decent standard of ethics. To allow a company the size of Theranos to operate in an active war zone on soldiers wounded in combat was out of the question.

Shoemaker, unfortunately, didn't know the person he was refusing and thought it odd that Holmes became hostile when he informed her of this. Holmes kept citing legal guidance she received from her lawyers but there were no lawyers present at the meeting. Neither did she have any correspondence to justify this statement. Holmes was visibly upset and duly cold-shouldered Shoemaker for the rest of the day.

Army procedure when it came to medical tests on troops is a thoroughly supervised process (Carreyrou, 2019). Any drug that is administered to troops has to pass FDA approval first. The first step is to set up an institutional review board (IRB) which would conduct drug tests under FDA approved guidelines while working closely with the agency. Only after IRB and FDA approval does the drug get released into battle. The procedure for all devices is the same.

In case of accelerated timelines brought on by emergencies, tests can be performed on leftover samples of soldiers. The results of these tests would not inform treatment of any current soldier, but would serve as a baseline to fast track IRB approval, which usually takes at least eight months.

None of this pleased Holmes and Shoemaker left the meeting with her assurances that she would find a solution. Shoemaker, for his part, got in touch with Jeremiah Kelly, a lawyer who was well-versed with FDA protocol and had his views confirmed. Holmes approached the duo requesting another meeting and this took place in December 2011 (Carreyrou, 2019).

Armed with a double-paged document, Holmes suggested a workaround that made both their heads spin. She justified this approach by citing legal backing from her lawyers, but then again, no lawyers were present. This was even more absurd because the meeting was being held at the offices of Theranos' counsel! Briefly, this was what Holmes proposed:

The medical devices were merely sample processing units that would submit the data back to Theranos' lab in Palo Alto. Decisions and diagnosis would be carried out in this lab and transmitted back to the devices, thus making them high tech messengers. The lab would be where the diagnosis would be carried out and thus, it was the lab that needed CLIA approval, which it already had. Given that the firm was already operating in the gray area, they did not need further FDA approval for the devices.

With Shoemaker firmly hanging on to his view that the FDA would take a dim view of all this, he reiterated to Holmes that Theranos would need to contact the IRB to determine an action plan to carry out the tests. Furthermore, she would also need FDA approval for either the devices or for the regulatory gray zone she thought was justified for Theranos.

Given her conviction and the pressure that was being applied from above at Central Command, Shoemaker began questioning his own sanity. As such, he decided to run this past his contacts at the FDA to check whether he was missing something.

Mad Dog And Shoemaker

In the summer of 2012, LTC Shoemaker received an email that jolted him awake and caused him to reconsider all his life choices up to that point. It was an email from his supervisor, LTC Edgar at Central Command and it was a forwarded chain of emails. The first email was from Holmes to James Mattis, himself, accusing Shoemaker of sabotaging Theranos and leaking false information to the FDA about the company's regulatory stance.

She vowed to get to the bottom of the matter and expressed surprise that people within the DOD were looking to sabotage Theranos' efforts. In response, Mattis had emailed Edgar, furious, and enquiring who "LTC Shoemaker" was, and "Why was he going around spreading false information?" Edgar in turn was asking Shoemaker what on Earth he was up to.

The fact was that the innocent email Shoemaker had sent to the FDA to check whether the regulatory structure Theranos was working under would fly for the Army's purposes, had taken on a life of its own. The person Shoemaker had sent the email to had forwarded it further down the line until it landed with the CMS.

All of a sudden, both agencies were made aware of the fact that this Silicon Valley startup they had never heard of was trying to exploit the very loophole that they frowned upon. Promptly, an inspector was dispatched to the main office in Palo Alto, much to Holmes and Balwani's chagrin. Upon reaching there, the inspector was surprised to discover that his visit wasn't particularly unexpected. Not only this, the pair even knew who had been responsible from central command for sending the inspector their way. Of course, this was never Shoemaker's intention since all he wanted to do was run a sanity check on what Theranos was proposing.

Turns out, during the email exchange, Shoemaker's boss, LTC Edgar, had emailed Holmes about Shoemaker's inquiry, thinking to keep her posted on how the Army was handling this matter. Either way, the inspector made it clear to Holmes that she could not legally deploy her analyzers under the umbrella of the CLIA certificate.

At this point, both Holmes and Balwani categorically denied that they had planned on doing this. The inspector thought this as odd. Why would a distinguished armed forces officer lie about something like this? The inspector was escorted to the lab - the East Meadow location having been shut down after Dupuy's departure - and he saw nothing out of the ordinary.

He didn't see any of Theranos' much vaunted analyzers either.

Balwani explained this was due to the fact that they were still under development. So how did they even pitch this to Mattis in the first place if everything was under development? The logical gymnastics that Holmes and Balwani were performing was getting too much for the inspector to stand.

However, there was nothing out of the ordinary with the lab and he had to be content with reminding the pair that there was no way they could operate the devices under the CLIA certificate. It was after this inspection - attack as far as Holmes was concerned - that she fired off the email to Mattis; Shoemaker and Edgar found themselves being ushered into Mattis' presence shortly thereafter (Carreyrou, 2019).

Mattis was frustrated with the lack of progress, and thanks to Holmes having framed it as the DOD's mistake, instead of the fact that Theranos had failed every step of the way, he was keen to get to the bottom of the bureaucratic tangle the devices found themselves in. Shoemaker, along with CMS inspector Alberto Gutierrez, explained the situation to the four-star general.

To his credit, Mattis saw the situation and looked for a quick solution to it. Gutierrez and Shoemaker proposed the emergency alternative, wherein leftover samples could be tested for validity, as the quickest way forward. Mattis agreed and Holmes found the ball back in her court.

To make it clear, gaining access to leftover samples was something even Shoemaker, during his long and distinguished career, had never achieved. He saw this as a once-in-a-lifetime opportunity. Indeed, even during his research on biological warfare and weaponized diseases, the DOD had never provided such level of access. Shoemaker thought it was a matter of time now for Theranos to get what it wanted. However, even on March 2013, when Mattis retired, Theranos hadn't yet begun. The following July, Shoemaker retired as well, the whole matter having long since been put to bed.

Chapter 7: Celebrity

By late 2013, Holmes was firmly out of the background and in the national spotlight. Thanks to a unique cocktail of tech company valuations, disruption, and the need for iconic female Silicon Valley CEOs, Holmes was able to maintain her façade as "the Steve Jobs of healthcare". Her fame would peak the following year.

As famous as she was, on the inside, Theranos was floundering. Indeed, the quality of Theranos as a company and Holmes' fame were inversely related. The miniLab would never see the light of day and Holmes would soon be forced to resort to even more questionable tactics in order to keep her lie going.

Balwani was busy terrorizing everyone on her behalf, the executioner to her judge, so to speak, despite not actually knowing a thing about either technology or medical science. While he certainly was knowledgeable with regards to coding, he was a genius only when compared to someone who had zero knowledge of computers. His claim of having written a million lines of code (Carreyrou, 2019) was quietly laughed at by the Theranos IT team.

While all of this was happening, the seeds of Theranos' unmasking were being sown. What started off as a, strangely, fully justified lawsuit Holmes had filed previously, would turn into her downfall. Everything with her was ironic, it seems. The one instance when she was in the right was what ultimately led to her downfall.

Patents And Lawsuits

In the world of Silicon Valley where a business is strangely not expected to make money, patents provide substantial protection. The strength of a firm is often determined by the number of patents it holds and like most valley firms, Theranos was no different. Employees had to agree to strict clauses and even a whiff of patent violation would result in a multitude of lawsuits.

Readers will recall the previous case of an employee who worked on a side project instead of working weekends. Holmes insisted the employee turn over the patent he was working on in order to continue his employment at Theranos, despite the patent having nothing to do with Theranos. In Holmes' world, this was fully justified. After all, she owned the employee, didn't she?

Another person who was very familiar with patents and could be equally as vindictive as Holmes was Richard Fuisz, the family friend of the Holmes'. Readers will recall from earlier chapters that Fuisz was a businessman who was well versed in the field of medical technology, aside from being a CIA operative in his earlier days.

To connect the dots fully, we will need to travel back to 2005, when Holmes had recently dropped out of Stanford and the Holmes had moved back to Washington D.C and reconnected with the Fuiszes.

Bruised Ego

Upon moving back to D.C, Lorraine Fuisz and Noel Holmes reconnected and resumed their warm friendship. Both were regular visitors to each other's homes and despite the frostiness that existed between their husbands, they got along swimmingly despite their vastly different backgrounds.

Elizabeth, at the time, was making headlines within the entrepreneurial world, with INC magazine profiling her alongside Mark Zuckerberg as the upcoming generation of visionaries to look out for. At this time, all Elizabeth had told her parents was her wearable patch idea from when she initially returned from her internship in Singapore.

While Theranos had long since moved on from this idea at the time, Noel Holmes was not to know this and boasted, as any proud mother would, to Lorraine Fuisz about Elizabeth's ideas and the recognition she was receiving. All of this was of massive interest to Richard Fuisz.

Unlike his wife who was content with being happy for the daughter of her friend, Fuisz decided to make it personal, like every situation he ever handled. Outraged at the fact that the daughter of his wife's close friend would decide to setup a company in the very field he was an expert in and not consult him, Fuisz decided to take a closer look at Theranos, in order to find some weakness.

His motivation may or may not have been to sabotage a then twenty-one-year-old's vision – only he can confirm this. Upon finding Holmes' patent, though, his opportunistic business side kicked in. Referring to the application along with an interview Holmes had given on NPR, Fuisz put two and two together and spotted an opportunity to profit from Theranos.

Readers will recall that Holmes' patch idea had two aspects to it. One was the diagnostic part, and the other was to send data to the physician in charge of administering drugs to the patient. By detecting adverse reactions to the drug within the patient, the device would transfer the data and alert the physician of this. Thanks to the way Holmes had filed her patent, there was an opening for Fuisz to exploit it if the device ever saw the light of day. Reasoning that the device would need to compare the existing data to the normal baseline for the patient, Fuisz filed a patent for a barcode to be inserted within the drug packaging which would contain the patient's baseline.

The device would scan the barcode and thus program itself to detect any deviations from the norm. This physician-alert device, as Fuisz put it, could embed itself onto any home testing medical device and relied only on existing technology. He even made it very clear who he as targeting, mentioning Theranos' proposed devices by name in the application as examples of potential customers.

The filing was with the USPTO on April 26, 2006 and would become public eighteen months later. Fuisz was careful to keep all of this to himself, working in the background while maintaining an outwardly friendly appearance with the Holmes. At one point he even suggested to Noel that he could help Elizabeth out with the specifics of the medical field and could assist Theranos in some manner.

Christian Holmes, never being a fan of Fuisz and fully knowing his neighbor's true nature, immediately heard alarm bells going off inside his head.

Shots Fired

Christian knew full well that one of Fuisz's sons, John, worked at the same firm that had helped Elizabeth file her first patent. Given the sudden interest Fuisz was showing in Theranos, it seemed logical to Christian that John had passed the information on to his father.

However, as we've seen, the reality was different. In addition to this, John wanted nothing to do with his father and the idea that he would jeopardize his career to help his father out is laughable. By this time, in 2008, Theranos had fully integrated the wireless communication aspect into their device, at least in idea form. Thus, it seemed to Christian that Fuisz had stolen Elizabeth's idea and patented it first, looking to profit.

In short, he had stolen the idea with the help of his son, John. With all this in mind, Christian approached Chuck Work, an old friend who happened to be the managing partner of the patent law firm in question. Work felt this was outlandish, knowing John, but looked into it anyway.

Given that John was a respected junior partner at the time and in good standing, Work didn't see any merit in this and advised Elizabeth and Christian that his firm was not in a position to represent them, given the complete lack of evidence against John Fuisz.

Elizabeth was undeterred and bided her time. Finally on October 29th 2011 (Carreyrou, 2019), Richard Fuisz was served with a notice of a lawsuit against his and his other son, Joe's, company. The name of the lawyer on the notice was David Boies. Boies had a reputation that preceded him, and by hiring his firm, Holmes had made it very clear she was not playing around.

Fuisz was expecting some sort of a reaction from Holmes all this while. His patent application had been approved and was registered in 2010. Once this happened, he made it a point to send news of this confirmation to Holmes via email, just to rub her face in it. Holmes would have to pay him royalties if she ever wanted Theranos' devices installed in people's homes from here on out.

Perhaps this explains Holmes' switch around this time, from wanting devices in every home to courting Walgreens and Safeway. Either way, she was going to give Fuisz everything he deserved and more, through the iron fist that was David Boies. Boies made his name during the antitrust lawsuits against Microsoft, where he famously deposed Bill Gates for twenty hours.

Boies had recently fought and overturned legislation against gay marriage in California and was a celebrity of sorts. In short, ruthless didn't even begin to describe Boies' approach. Richard, Joe and John soon found this out when they discovered they were under surveillance, thanks to their neighbors, and spotting cars following them when they drove around.

John was an unwilling participant in all of this and his father's actions made him collateral damage. Boies knew perfectly well that John had nothing to do with all of this but still did his best to tarnish his reputation in an effort to paint him as being dishonest. As mentioned earlier, there are no heroes in this story.

Thankfully for John, the judge threw out the claims against him in court at which point Boies filed once again in the state court in Washington D.C. The judge in D.C threw the claim out as well. Despite this setback, the lawsuit against Richard and Joe remained valid since the patent was owned by the firm they owned together.

John was, however, not completely off the hook. He had left his old law firm to begin his new practice but was now facing problems thanks to the allegations Boies had made previously. His opposing counsel often brought this up and he was having problems signing clients. Thus John, who had a short fuse, looked at the main lawsuit as a vendetta against Holmes and even testified in a deposition that he would do his absolute best to sabotage Holmes as long as he was alive (Carreyrou, 2019).

The elder Fuisz, whose fault all of this was, meanwhile, was alarmed at the rising legal cost of defending the case. It seemed obvious that he should have thought of this earlier. Either way, he soon decided to switch law firms, choosing cheaper options, and began conducting research on his own.

Given that Holmes was a college dropout with no scientific training whatsoever, it made sense that Theranos' patents were worked on by scientists within the organization and Holmes' name was simply a placeholder. Fuisz noticed one particular name, Ian Gibbons, that kept surfacing. With an intention of turning to Gibbons, Fuisz set about trying to get in touch with him.

Thus, the seeds of Holmes' downfall were sown. While the lawsuit rumbled on in the background, out of sight to everyone except the protagonists, Holmes and Theranos were climbing to greater heights in the public eye.

Branding

Around the time Steve Burd was on his way out of Safeway and Mattis was retiring from his position in the armed forces, Holmes was busy preparing her public image along with that of Theranos'. She was reading the signs and given her rapport with Mattis, who still thought the world of her despite repeated delays; it was obvious that her becoming a celebrity on par with her idol Jobs was just a matter of time.

To this effect, she hired the ad agency Chiat\Day during the spring of 2013. The agency was responsible for a number of successful ad campaigns for Apple and had long been the go-to firm for valley companies, if they had the pedigree. Holmes and Balwani soon began discussions with the agency representatives and initial brand concepts were developed.

Advertising Misgivings

Holmes' relationship with the ad agency played out much the same way as every other relationship of hers. The higher ups, invariably older men, in this case a man named Patrick O'Neill, were smitten with her, and the people actually doing the work and dealing with her on a day-to-day basis felt extremely nervous about her claims.

Chiat\Day had more than just its reputation to worry about. Given that Theranos was a medical device company, the agency was legally liable for any false claims made on any of Theranos' branding. The first task the agency was presented with was a website redesign.

Up until that point, the Theranos website had a rudimentary look to it, without much branding or a coherent message. This was not an oversight on Holmes' part; just that it wasn't a priority. Her first step was to schedule creative meetings on Wednesdays since she had heard this was what Apple did (Carreyrou, 2019).

The executives assigned to the account considered Holmes initially as someone a bit idealistic and perhaps naive. Holmes had the charisma of someone who was on a mission and given her spiel about reducing deaths worldwide and building disease maps, it was easy to convince the executives that creating branding for Theranos went beyond the usual aim of just marketing. Holmes was changing the world and there was no doubt about it.

However, there was the fact that Holmes and Balwani were a package deal. Much like everyone else he encountered, Balwani made everyone uneasy, even when he thought he was being charming. He used a ton of software jargon with the ad execs (Carreyrou, 2019) which was not really relevant to the topic at hand.

Furthermore, for someone who had sold a company during the height of the dot-com boom, it seemed odd that he had managed to leave zero traces of himself on the web. Other valley entrepreneurs didn't really know who he was and he hadn't dedicated himself to anything else after his initial windfall.

Balwani was not shy, though. When quizzed about revenue projections and sales figures, he leaned on the optimistic side. When pressed to reveal his sources, his answers were either vague or he flipped back to quoting software jargon, much like he'd blame the "wireless" for the Edisons' lack of results.

He routinely clashed with the executives over payment, often demanding a line-by-line accounting of Chiat\Day's bills. At an annual retainer cost of $6 million per year, a lot of the execs wondered where Theranos was getting the money from (Carreyrou, 2019). Holmes routinely mentioned that the firm's black boxes were being used by the military in Afghanistan. This caused some execs to wonder whether Theranos was a front for the military or the CIA.

The paranoia was something else that struck the executives on the ground as odd. Accustomed to working for valley startups, they were used to maintaining secrecy for their clients, but Theranos took things to another level. It is easy to understand now why this was. Theranos had not even a single working product at this point in time and the best way to conceal it was to paint an elaborate picture around it and distract everyone's gaze.

Holmes insisted that every document Theranos sent Chiat\Day's way be numbered and filed separately in the agency's head office, separate from its other clients. The documents would not be disposed of by the agency, but instead be sent back to Theranos on request. All material would be printed on a dedicated printer which would be present within this locked room and no one except the executives assigned to the account would have access.

Given the hyperbolic claims Holmes was making, the executives pressed for proof of the fact that the analyzers worked. Their first point of contact was Chris Holmes and his frat pack, referred to as "Therabros" (Carreyrou, 2019) by the execs. Unable to receive a straight answer from them, Balwani and Holmes were next in line. They sent Chiat\Day a password-protected file which contained what they claimed were excerpts of a study conducted by Johns Hopkins certifying the black boxes.

This was the same study that Hunter had previously laughed at when Walgreens had presented it to him. Holmes was careful this time about disguising the document to make it look far more substantial. The launch date for the website had to be delayed repeatedly because of the back and forth over the claims Holmes was making.

Finally, a tentative go-live time happened somewhere in September 2013. This month was crucial for Theranos because, unbeknownst to everyone except Holmes and Balwani, they had earmarked the 9th as the date to go live within Walgreens (Carreyrou, 2019). By this point, Burd had retired from Safeway and the Pentagon project was going nowhere.

Walgreens had been waiting for three years at this point, and if Holmes could not deliver, they were liable to walk, their inferiority complex to CVS be damned. This marked the beginning of the final phase of fraud that Holmes would commit and it would coincide with her becoming a national celebrity.

For now, though, the Chiat\Day executives struggled with website copy and branding slogans. Holmes had brought out of storage something called a "nanotainer", which would house the tiny drop of blood collected from patients. The ad execs were excited by this, thanks to the marketable name and the visual impact it had, being less than the size of a dime.

Then, out of the blue, the evening before the website was to go live (Carreyrou, 2019), Holmes and Balwani scheduled an emergency meeting where they went over each and every line of the website copy. The head honcho at Chiat\Day, O'Neill, thought of it as a routine valley company act but to those who had practical experience working with Holmes throughout this while, it was obvious she was dialing down her claims of what Theranos could do.

As John Carreyrou records in his book, *Bad Blood* (Carreyrou, 2019):

"Welcome to a revolution in lab testing" was changed to "Welcome to Theranos." "Faster results. Faster answers" became "Fast results. Fast answers." "A tiny drop is all it takes" was now "A few drops is all it takes."

A blurb of text next to the photo of a blond-haired, blue-eyed toddler under the headline "Goodbye, big bad needle" had previously referred only to finger-stick draws. Now it read, "Instead of a huge needle, we can use a tiny finger stick or collect a micro-sample from a venous draw."

In a part of the site entitled "Our Lab," a banner running across the page beneath an enlarged photo of a nanotainer had stated, "At Theranos, we can perform all of our lab tests on a sample 1/$_{1,000}$ the size of a typical blood draw." In the new version of the banner, the words "all of" were gone.

Under the heading "Unrivaled accuracy," it cited the statistic of about 93 percent of lab errors being caused by humans and inferred from it that "no other laboratory is more accurate than Theranos." Sure enough, that was walked back too.

September 7th, 2013

On September 7th, 2013, which was a Saturday, Elizabeth Holmes officially planted herself into the public's consciousness. As part of the *Wall Street Journal*'s Weekend Interview feature, Holmes occupied the front page of the venerable publication. Likening the process of drawing blood via a syringe as "vampirism" (Carreyrou, 2019), the author went on to profile Holmes by describing how she was anointed the "next Steve Jobs or Bill Gates."

This endorsement came from none other than George Shultz, the former secretary of state, A.K.A the man who ended the Cold War. Theranos' process involved "microscopic quantities" of blood and were "faster, cheaper and better" than traditional methods (Carreyrou, 2019).

Theranos' machines were being rolled out in Walgreens stores at that time of writing, and the world was on the cusp of a medical revolution – all thanks to the brilliant, young Stanford dropout. (Carreyrou, 2019)

Chapter 8: A Crisis Within

Richard Fuisz's entire case seemingly rested on his ability to turn Ian Gibbons around and to get the scientist to testify that his patent had nothing to do with Theranos' initial forays into medical testing. While it is doubtful that his claim was fully true, there is no doubt about the fact that Gibbons would never otherwise have testified against Theranos or Holmes and Balwani.

This was not out of loyalty, but due to the fear that had been instilled in him. A career scientist and an extremely accomplished one at that, Gibbons fit every stereotype of a nerdy scientist. As Holmes' celebrity grew, Fuisz was doing his best to uncover details about this reclusive scientist within Theranos.

Team Management

Gibbons was one of the first employees to join Theranos, joining as far back as 2005 when Holmes' vision was, perhaps, still sincere and her lies hadn't overtaken her. He was a close friend of the first man Holmes had hoodwinked – Stanford's Channing Robertson. Robertson had recommended Gibbons to Holmes in order to head the fledgling company's biochemistry team.

It was an uneasy relationship from the start.

Demotions And Apathy

Gibbons' specialty was immunoassays and as a result, the first iterations of Theranos' products focused on these types of tests. Having worked previously at a number of prestigious labs, Gibbons found the communication restrictions placed between his and the engineering teams ridiculous (Carreyrou, 2019).

Holmes' justification of this via the trade secrecy pretext also made no sense to him. Thus, he faced the same problems developing the 1.0 as Edmond Ku did and later Tony Nugent would. Nugent and Gibbons couldn't be kept apart forever, and once the Edison was built to a decent degree, the two promptly began to butt heads over the direction the device ought to take.

Gibbons placed a high premium on quality and insisted that the quality of the test results from the devices be on par with results obtained by a chemist on a bench, i.e. the old fashioned way. This seems like a logical thing to desire and it isn't entirely clear why Nugent would object to this, not being anywhere near as big a liar as Holmes is.

Either way, early on in his tenure at Theranos, Gibbons was demoted from the team lead position of the biochemistry group and was effectively its number two. While this was a blow for him personally, he took it in stride since he believed in the vision Holmes laid out and relished the challenge the work presented.

Much like how Shaunak Roy was disappointed with the switch from the microfluidics based 1.0 to the more conventional Edison, Gibbons was as well. This caused him to take a second look at where the company was headed and not for the first time, he found himself uncomfortable with the way Holmes was stretching the truth.

Billion Dollar Facade

In reality, Holmes had left the truth a long way behind but even in the segregated and paranoid workplace that was Theranos, some information managed to filter through. His rising unease moved him to call his old friend Robertson and let him know what was going on.

Instead of listening to his old friend, Robertson did what every other besotted elder gentleman exposed to Holmes has done thus far. He let Holmes know everything that Gibbons was telling him about, and shortly, Gibbons found himself demoted once again. This demotion was a relief for Gibbons because Holmes had originally fired him but upon his colleagues' insistence, Gibbons was rehired and given another chance.

Eventually, though, the demotion began to squeeze on him mainly due to the fact that he was now a consultant working under a man whom he had hired just a couple months previously. Meanwhile, looking around at Theranos, it seemed as if Holmes was moving on from the older guard of employees who had brought her what little results she could boast of.

Gibbons' once arch enemy ,Nugent, found himself sidelined thanks to the non-existent miniLab, and with the Edison still limited and unreliable, Nugent and Gibbons began to connect over their shared misfortune. When the move to the newest offices happened - Facebook's old location - Gibbons found himself stuck on a nondescript desk within the general area, far away from any relevant lab work.

He was still consulted on the development of the miniLab but his inputs were long being ignored by Balwani and Holmes. Despondent, he took to working from home most of the time. Another complication in all of this was the fact that Gibbons had been diagnosed with colon cancer in 2007. He was in remission by 2013 but thanks to the secretive nature of their workplace, his colleagues assumed it was the cancer that was waylaying him.

Once the Fuisz case gathered steam, Gibbons was notified that he would have to testify on Theranos' behalf, given that most of its patents had his name on it. Implicit within this request was the fact that he would be expected to denounce Fuisz's patent as a copy of Theranos', but Gibbons was not comfortable with this.

However, the fact was that at the age of sixty-seven, Gibbons felt he would not be able to find alternative employment and needed the job security Theranos offered. He contacted Holmes in order to discuss the issue. When Holmes promptly responded back with a meeting date for the very next day, Gibbons feared some sort of retribution. The very same day, he received a call from Theranos' lawyers asking him to come into the office.

Convinced he no longer had a future at the firm and seeing no hope for his prospects going forward, on May 16th, in the early hours of dawn Gibbons downed a fatal dose of Tylenol along with a bottle of wine. His intention to commit suicide worked and on May 23rd, he was pronounced dead, leaving behind his grieving wife, Rochelle.

Holmes wrote an email to a small group of Theranos employees informing them of this tragedy and mentioned something about conducting a memorial service. She never broached the subject again beyond this.

It was left to Gibbons' one-time enemy, Nugent, to paste all the patents Gibbons had developed for Theranos onto an email and circulate them to a small list of colleagues, as a reminder of Gibbons' immense contribution to the firm. This was the only memorial Gibbons received. Most of the firm believed he had passed away from cancer.

Endofactors

All this while, Balwani and Holmes were scrambling to meet the Walgreens deadline. They desperately tried changing course with the miniLab, now deciding to operate it in much the same way as they had operated the Edisons for Safeway. Instead of placing them within the stores, they would have Walgreens courier them samples and test them in-house.

With the miniLab nowhere near complete, the stress of it all was getting to Balwani. By now, the large H-1B contingent at Theranos gave him free reign to terrorize whoever he wanted. Reportedly, Balwani would often stroll by at 7:30PM through the engineering section to make sure everyone there was working.

Given this dynamic and their penchant for firing anyone who disagreed with them, Holmes and Balwani were now surrounded by a bunch of yes men whose primary job it was to agree with everything they said and obey their every order unquestioningly. The H1 employees didn't really have much of a choice since it was either this or head back to their home countries and the attendant lack of opportunity.

A few of them did employ novel coping methods though. One particular engineer figured out that the best way to keep Balwani off his back was to reply to his emails with even longer, more than five hundred word, emails. Balwani didn't have the patience to read them through, but given the length, would assume some work was being done (Carreyrou, 2019).

Another tactic was to schedule regular meetings and invite Balwani. After attending the first few, he would lose interest and stop attending. The teams also played on his ignorance and ego quite a bit.

One particular meeting, Balwani reportedly misheard the term "end effector" for "endofactor".

The next meeting was titled "Endofactors Update" (Carreyrou, 2019) and Balwani sat through all of it with the engineering team laughing behind his back. They played word games with him, trying to get him to use made-up words or words out of context. Balwani remained oblivious to it all and continued to behave as if he knew everything.

Hacking

There were a number of problems with the miniLab and the biggest of them all was that it was incapable of processing more than one sample at a time. This made Theranos' ambition to process patient samples from multiple locations a complete joke because commercial blood analyzers at the time could process several at once. Indeed, this is why all of them were bigger in size.

With Holmes' marketing focused on the drop of blood Theranos would need, increasing the size of the miniLab was out of the question. Therefore, Holmes did what she knew best – cheat. She decided to launch the Walgreens venture with the Edison and meanwhile, tasked one of her employees with hacking an existing commercial blood analyzer.

This employee was none other than Daniel Young, the previously mentioned appendage on the Mexico studies whose job it was to build mathematical models. Since then, thanks to relentless sycophancy, he had risen to a position where he was a step below only Holmes and Balwani.

The machine they chose to hack was an ADVIA 1800, made by

Siemens healthcare. The ADVIA specialized in general chemistry assays and Holmes reasoned that between the immunoassays from the Edison and the rest from the ADVIA, Theranos could cover the majority of tests promised.

The ADVIA needed to be hacked, however, to make it compatible with micro-sized samples like the ones Theranos would be collecting. Young and another colleague modified the machine to do this by diluting the samples with a larger amount of saline solution. By doing this, the volume of liquid entering the ADVIA remained the same, even if the blood concentration was lower than normal.

There was just one problem: The lower concentration of blood lowered the concentration of analytes in the blood below the approved specification range for the machine. This made using the ADVIA with these concentration levels illegal and outright fraudulent.

Holmes didn't particularly care about this, given the deadline that was fast approaching. She duly purchased ten more ADVIAs. Meanwhile, given the fact that the Edisons were still malfunctioning and with this new development, the head of the immunoassays group had quit. Her resignation was not acknowledged within the company and the rumor mill only intensified.

A Crucial Hire

During early 2013, Holmes hired Alan Beam to head lab operations at Theranos. In his new role, he would be in charge of the general chemistry assays and as such, in charge of the biological side of the ill-fated miniLabs. Beam was soon struck by the despondent attitude of staff within the lab. Like everyone else, he had been sold on

Theranos' vision by Holmes and her giddy optimism.

The lab itself was divided into two parts – one upstairs and one downstairs. The upstairs portion was CLIA certified and contained the commercial blood analyzers. Downstairs is where the miniLabs were. Beam was further surprised to find out that the miniLabs were nowhere close to working and that the nanotainers, so prominent in their advertising, routinely shattered within the machine and that the samples within it were contaminated frequently.

Beam then watched in horror as the ADVIA machines were hacked and jail-broken by Young on Holmes' orders. He was well aware of the upcoming Walgreens deadline and knew what was about to happen: Patient samples were going to be run on the illegally-modified machines.

Soon after the Walgreens launch was live, accompanied by the front page profile of Holmes in the Journal, Beam had another headache to deal with. The CLIA license for Theranos' lab was expiring and an inspector from the local state authority would be stopping by for an inspection. Balwani made it clear to Beam that the downstairs portion of the lab was not to be shown to the inspector.

Beam compromised on this outright fraud by simply not pointing out that a downstairs portion even existed to the inspector, trying to convince himself he wasn't committing fraud. However, he wasn't so sure deep down (Carreyrou, 2019). As for Walgreens, the tests that were being carried out on the jail-broken ADVIAs were from samples of venous draws, so the dilution wasn't an issue.

Yet, Balwani soon ordered finger pinprick blood draws for a number of tests that would be carried out on the ADVIAs. Beam pleaded his case to Holmes, trying to get her to see that the results from such tests would be blatantly wrong and that Theranos could not simply make up results and lie about it. He even went as far as banning the release of certain results which indicated a level of Potassium below a threshold to patients. Holmes responded by sending Young to "fix" the results and the assay.

Beam wasn't at breaking point yet. However, what was happening to him was one of a number of parallel events that would eventually expose Holmes for the liar she is. It would all erupt in less than two years' time.

Victory

Richard Fuisz was being forced to admit defeat. Never one who was able to set aside his emotions when making decisions, he and his son Joe had long since taken to representing themselves in their case against Theranos. Joe, being a patent lawyer, they felt, was more than qualified to take on this case.

This was a bit like Fuisz fielding a kindergarten team against the Yankees All-Star lineup that was David Boies and his firm. Shortly, Fuisz was forced to come to terms with the fact that he would have to settle and had zero shot at winning this case. Even worse, what had put him in this position was the fact that Boies had cleverly trapped him into uttering certain inconsistencies in court and then correctly gambled that Fuisz's ego would not allow him to backtrack.

Thus, the elder Fuisz was caught in a trap of his own making and would have been better off literally shoving a boot in his mouth. Then there was the coup de grace of Fuisz claiming Theranos was never the target of his patent despite Theranos being mentioned clearly in the application. Ian Gibbons' death had robbed what little hope they had, and despite developing a relationship based on a shared hatred of Holmes with his widow, Rochelle, Fuisz was lucky Boies even considered settling.

After one final, veiled threat to destroy John, who had nothing to do with this whole affair, Boies offered a deal to Fuisz, which the latter accepted gratefully (Carreyrou, 2019). He was defeated. He remains the only person to go into a lawsuit against Holmes and actually end up looking worse than her – justifiably so.

In the larger picture though, the best thing to come out of this whole mess was the insight Fuisz gained from Rochelle and the tentative anti-Holmes network that was being born.

The Statesman

If James Mattis offered Holmes' entry into the big leagues, George Shultz was the one who cemented her place there. A former secretary of state under the Nixon administration, this was the man who stared down champions of communism from across a table and had helped end the Cold War. As skilled a negotiator and judge of human character as he was, he found Holmes one of the most impressive people he had ever met.

It is not fully clear how the pair met, but thanks to Shultz's residence in Stanford, it couldn't have been all too hard for Holmes to find an audience with the elder statesman. It was Shultz who had paved the way for Holmes to appear on the front page of the *WSJ*. He joined the Theranos' board in July 2011, and during his time there, actively recruited a number of fellow luminaries into the company.

Billion Dollar Facade

In late 2011, Shultz's grandson Tyler, who was then a student at Stanford, met Holmes at his grandfather's home, and was carried away by Holmes' vision for her company and the world. After a summer internship at the company, he joined full time and was assigned to the immunoassay team. On his first day on the job, the head of the team quit. This was around the time when Alan Beam was witnessing first-hand the fraud that was happening inside the labs.

Soon, Tyler Shultz befriended a fellow recent graduate named Erika Cheung and both of them were assigned with the task of verifying the accuracy of the Edison's test results. Shultz shortly found himself staring at the insides of an Edison and was profoundly disappointed to see that there was nothing ground-breaking about it. It had a clunky touchscreen interface and a robotic arm on the inside which was prone to breaking the pipettes attached to it.

Furthermore, Shultz and Cheung soon found that Theranos employees were cherry-picking data in order to present the Edison in a more favorable light. In one particular test to detect Syphilis, a simple yes/no result, the Edison detected only 65% of the cased in one run and 80% in a second. However, a final report went out mentioning 95% as the success rate (Carreyrou, 2019).

Then there were repeated failures to detect levels of Vitamin D accurately, with the Edison regularly implying a deficiency in healthy samples. Despite all of this, the device was cleared to do analysis of live samples from actual patients. Shortly thereafter, Cheung was moved effectively to ground zero, the downstairs lab where the miniLab was being developed.

Here, Cheung was tasked with performing QA on the miniLab's test results and again she found repeated failures. However, under the instruction of Daniel Young, Cheung witnessed an R&D employee who was not CLIA-licensed walk in and perform an analysis and hand over appropriate data to be reported. All Cheung could do was stare in horror (Carreyrou, 2019).

Soon, she was joined by Shultz in the downstairs lab.

Billionaire

Meanwhile, the *WSJ* article had not gone unnoticed. With interest rates at rock bottom and the entire stock market in a bull run which would last the entire decade, the markets were flush with money. Hedge funds which prided themselves on outperforming the broader market were finding it harder to do so, given the nosebleed levels the market was heading towards.

Thus, hedge funds were more willing than ever to go outside their box and look to the valley for investment ideas. Theranos seemed a perfect play to such investors and soon Holmes fielded a call from Partner Fund Management, a hedge fund based in San Francisco run by Christopher James and Brian Grossman (Carreyrou, 2019).

The first thing that the pair noticed upon arriving at the headquarters was the paranoia that greeted them. There were security guards everywhere and they were escorted everywhere they went, including to the restroom. Holmes had convinced herself that her competitors, LabCorp and Quest, were out to undermine Theranos and were actively plotting industrial espionage against her company.

In reality, it is doubtful that the two established companies had even heard of what Theranos was up to. Mattis had recently joined the board of the company, and forgetting that Palo Alto wasn't Afghanistan, his choice for head of security was ratcheted up several points. The paranoia made a positive impression on the hedge fund pair, though.

Reminded of Coca Cola's efforts to protect the Coke recipe, they reasoned Theranos had similarly valuable IP to protect and were fully bought into the story they were being pitched. Holmes and Balwani told the pair that the devices developed by Theranos were able to perform a large majority of tests, identified by special codes labs used to bill insurers. Theranos apparently had the ability to perform 1000 of the 1300 codes with just a pinprick of blood from the patient (Carreyrou, 2019).

Next, a scatter plot showing the correlation of Theranos' results to those commercially available was shown. The plot showed a tightly clustered array of dots around a rising forty-five degree line which indicated that the company's results were very closely related to those commercially available.

The underlying data for this plot was based on results from the commercial analyzers Theranos had purchased, and not the miniLab nor the Edison devices. One wonders why Holmes simply didn't make up data since she was so well accustomed to lying about everything at this point. Besides, she soon lied about the fact that Theranos' devices and tests were in the process of FDA approval when, in fact, nothing of the sort had taken place.

The final nail in the coffin for the doomed hedge fund duo was when they took a look at the board of Theranos. It was an intimidating list. There were Shultz and Mattis. Henry Kissinger, never too far away from a controversy, was there. William Perry, former secretary of defence, Sam Nunn the former chairman of the senate arms services committee and Gary Roughead, former navy admiral, rounded out the list (Carreyrou, 2019).

Holmes and Balwani soon sent the investment geniuses a spreadsheet containing revenue projections. The 2014 revenue was projected at $261 million with a bottom line of $165 million. 2015 was projected at an absurd $1.68 billion with a bottom line of $1.08 billion. You'd think they would have noticed the lack of a CFO at Theranos, given the sort of research hedge funds would usually perform prior to investment (Carreyrou, 2019).

Indeed, once Mosley had departed, Holmes hadn't bothered with hiring a CFO and Balwani performed the role as best as he could, which is to say, he took every opportunity to lie. Either way, the hedge fund pair noticed the presence of David Boies on the board as well and reasoned that the prestigious lawyer would surely have been keeping an eye on things.

On February 4th, 2014, Partner Fund paid $96 million and purchased 5,655,294 shares of Theranos at a price of $17 per share. This implied an astonishing valuation of $9 billion. Holmes, who owned half the company, now had a net worth north of $5 billion.

Peak

Once Richard Fuisz agreed to Boies' settlement offer, the matter was reported in the newsletter, Litigation Daily, and this caught the attention of Roger Parloff, the legal correspondent for Fortune magazine. The story was unusual in that Boies had personally taken part in the defense instead of handing the case over to one of his associates.

Then there was Fuisz on the other side who had settled this all of a sudden and his son John who had vowed vengeance on Holmes. It seemed a juicy story and Parloff got in touch with the PR rep for

Boies and soon was being pitched a story about the company involved, Theranos, itself.

Parloff hadn't read the *WSJ* interview of Holmes or the shortly-published piece about her on Wired and Boies' enthusiasm for this relatively unknown young woman intrigued him further. Thus, dropping the legal angle of the case, he set out to do a story on Holmes herself.

Holmes dangled a carrot in front of him by mentioning that Theranos had a valuation of over $9 billion. When Parloff questioned the medical authenticity of Theranos' machines, Holmes was evasive but these concerns were put to rest by the besotted, powerful old men on the board of Theranos and their effusive praise of her.

Thus, Parloff ran his story and Holmes made the cover of Fortune magazine with the title "This CEO is out for blood" (Carreyrou, 2019). This catapulted her into national consciousness. Soon, Holmes was presenting her vision at a TEDMED talk where she brought out her nanotainer and despite not giving any specifics about what Theranos actually did, managed to win over the audience.

During all of these appearances, she talked up her phobia of needles and made that a justification for Theranos' pinprick system. She mentioned one of her main motivations for creating disease maps and for predicting the rise of malignant diseases to be the loss of her uncle, Ron Dietz, to cancer. No one bothered to notice that she hadn't even bothered to check up on her uncle even once during this time.

Further articles and magazine covers followed. Holmes was featured in *Forbes*, USA today, INC, Fast Company, *Glamour*, NPR, Fox Business, CNN, CNBC and CBS. Harvard Medical School invited her to become part of its board of medical fellows. She was appointed a US Ambassador for global entrepreneurship and one of *Time* magazine's Most Influential People in the World. To cap it all off, she won the Horatio Alger award. By October 20th, 2014, her net worth was estimated to be $4.5 billion (Carreyrou, 2019).

This would be Holmes' peak – the final moment when her lies hadn't yet overtaken her facade. Given the level of fame and adulation she achieved, it was just a matter of time now before it all went tumbling down. The lies were too big and she was in too deep. The only way out was to dig deeper.

Thus, she doubled down on her lies and unleashed a terrifying assault on anyone who dared oppose her from here on out.

Chapter 9: Unmasking

Tyler Shultz rejoined Erika Cheung in the downstairs laboratory in early 2014 and both bore further witness to the active fraud that was being carried out. By this point in time, Balwani had expressly instructed staff to screen the jail-broken ADVIAs from Siemens staff who swung by to perform maintenance on the other machines Theranos had purchased.

Just as Theranos hit its $9 billion valuation, Shultz was debating whether to inform his grandfather of all this or not. The old man treated Holmes like a daughter and Shultz wasn't sure whether to bust his bubble.

Either way, he figured he'd give Holmes the benefit of the doubt and attended Holmes' birthday party at his grandfather's house.

Retribution

The birthday party resembled a gathering of a queen and her admirers, with Holmes the center of attention. The party was attended by the majority of Theranos' board and she soaked up all the attention she was receiving. Not a bad way to hit thirty years of age, all in all.

Tyler Shultz still felt himself to be on good enough terms with Holmes to notify her of what he was witnessing in the labs below and soon sent an email requesting a meeting. During this meeting, he listed his concerns to her and Holmes claimed to be unaware of what was happening. She brushed aside his concerns, however, and asked him to speak to Daniel Young about it.

Shultz went into this second meeting thinking he was about to receive answers. Instead, he had stepped over the line and was about to enter a world of pain.

Betrayal

Young had a rebuttal for every single one of Shultz's objections, except that every single rebuttal followed the sort of gray area reasoning that Holmes had perfected, much like the regulatory structure that Theranos was operating under. Unconvinced with all of this and with full confirmation of illegality going on within Theranos, as a last ditch effort, Shultz thought of appealing to his grandfather, who was, after all, a board member and deserved to know what was going on.

Before doing this, though, Shultz sent an email to the New York State department of health to verify whether the manner in which Theranos was conducting its proficiency testing (a federal requirement labs have to satisfy) was legal. He had sent the email using an alias and was glad he had done so upon reading the response that Theranos was in gross violation of state and federal law.

Armed with this, Tyler approached his grandfather. The elder Shultz unfortunately didn't really understand what his grandson was talking about. While well versed in politics, none of the board at Theranos was qualified to perform the job that a board of directors is supposed to do. That is, they wielded significant clout and authority in their respective fields but none of them knew anything about running a business, let alone a highly specialized biotechnology firm.

The days of qualified people like Avie Tevanian occupying board positions were long gone; Holmes had seen to that. His grandfather decided on giving Holmes another chance to explain herself and thus, Tyler sent a long email with all of his findings to Holmes. This time, Balwani replied accusing Shultz of sullying the firm's reputation and demanded an apology without actually addressing any of the points Tyler had made.

Shultz responded instead with his resignation letter and signed the necessary confidentiality agreements and walked away. As he was doing so, he received a frantic call from his mother telling him that Holmes had called his grandfather and had given Tyler a warning. If he didn't stop his vendetta against her company, he would pay the price (Carreyrou, 2019).

Shocked, Tyler met his grandfather and explained the situation to him. The elder Shultz listened and calmly told Tyler that he (Tyler) was wrong.

With Shultz gone, Erika Cheung knew she had no place in the firm as well. Alarmed at the Edisons being cleared for Hepatitis C testing, Cheung had recently refused to conduct a test on a sample she had received. Breaking down, she notified her supervisors of her intention to quit (Carreyrou, 2019).

This didn't sit well with Balwani who berated her before accepting her request. On the way out, she was warned by HR not to post anything about Theranos on social media. She was further warned that the company had ways of tracking everything she did (Carreyrou, 2019).

Beam Breaks

As head of Theranos' labs, Alan Beam was well aware of everything Tyler and Cheung were observing. Manipulated test results, false and misleading statements to regulators and now to top it all, Beam had to field numerous calls from doctors complaining about the test results. His job, on Balwani's orders, was to convince the doctors that the results were correct despite knowing they were false.

While he was uncomfortable doing this for Vitamin D tests, he was scandalized when Balwani expected him to do the same for results of infectious diseases, much like Cheung had done. Unable to bear the strain, he quit. On his resignation email to Balwani and Holmes, he requested his name be removed from the CLIA license and that he would serve a month's notice if need be till they found a replacement.

Beam had long since been forwarding work emails to his personal account in order to gather evidence. Anticipating trouble, he wanted adequate protection for himself. He returned after a couple weeks of vacationing to the office to be met by Balwani and HR. Balwani was fully aware of the emails he had been forwarding to his personal address and mentioned that, along with signing a non-disclosure affidavit, he would need to allow HR into his personal account and delete those emails.

Beam flatly refused and walked out. Promptly, he began receiving threatening messages from Boies' law firm, Boies Schiller, and upon seeing what he was up against, hired a lawyer. However, this lawyer was also intimidated by the powerful law firm and Beam was forced to delete all work emails from his personal account.

There was only one record left with which Beam could protect himself. He had previously emailed a law firm out in Washington

D.C, which was famous for handling whistle-blower cases – a chain of eighteen emails as proof of wrongdoing. However, that firm hadn't confirmed whether he had a case or not. He got in touch with them in the hope of having them retrieve those emails.

Fuisz On The Hunt

Despite having suffered defeat, the research process which Richard Fuisz undertook left him feeling extremely skeptical of Theranos' claims of breakthrough technology. Unable to digest his loss to Holmes, Fuisz began gathering what he saw as evidence of Holmes' wrongdoing.

His first step was to get in touch with Phyllis Gardner, a professor at Stanford and a long time friend. Gardner had been consulted by Holmes during the patch idea days and had earned Holmes' ire by suggesting it wouldn't work. Given this initial experience with Holmes, Gardner was skeptical that a college dropout without a medical or biological background could produce something ground-breaking.

Meanwhile, Fuisz also got in touch with Rochelle Gibbons and given what she added, Fuisz realized something was very wrong at Theranos. He didn't have any conclusive proof, however, thanks to Ian Gibbons' tragic suicide. Meanwhile, Holmes was profiled in *The New Yorker* in December 2014 in an article which ran along the same lines as the previous *Fortune* article.

This article, to its credit, did pose some uncomfortable questions. First, there was a quote from a Quest scientist who felt finger prick samples would not be enough to produce accurate results (Carreyrou, 2019). Second, the lack of peer reviewed research. Holmes had quoted a paper published in a journal named *Hematology Reports* as a rebuttal to this.

Fuisz then came across a blog, entitled *Pathology Blawg*, run by Dr. Adam Clapper, a practicing pathologist who had posted his reaction to the New Yorker story. After registering his skepticism, he then pointed out that *Hematology Reports* was an online-only publication to which anyone who paid a $500 fee could publish to. Furthermore, the study Holmes had authored included data for just six patients.

Fuisz immediately got in touch with Clapper and filled him in on what he knew already, thanks to Rochelle Gibbons and Gardner, along with his own experiences. Clapper, however, felt that it was all a bit circumstantial. A few days later, Fuisz received a notification of someone having viewed his LinkedIn profile.

It was Alan Beam.

Enter Carreyrou

Fuisz didn't know Beam personally but noticed his job title and messaged him immediately, urging him to talk. Beam and Fuisz eventually spoke on the phone along with Gibbons and Gardner, and Theranos' worst secrets came spilling out. However, Beam was terrified of being found out.

Boies Schiller's lawyers were hounding him on a daily basis at this point and he was petrified at the thought of being sued. Fuisz appreciated his viewpoint and didn't press him further. Armed with this new information, Fuisz got back in touch with Clapper and presented the facts as they were.

Clapper, being an amateur blogger, didn't have the resources to follow up on the story or the skill. He knew someone at the *Wall Street Journal* who did, though. This reporter and he had worked previously on an investigative piece on medical malpractice and Clapper assured Fuisz he would get in touch with him. And thus, this was how John Carreyrou got wind of Theranos and Elizabeth Holmes.

Carreyrou, a French-American, was and is a distinguished journalist and a two time Pulitzer-prize winner. He won his first Pulitzer in explanatory reporting, in 2002, for a series of stories for the *WSJ* on corporate scandals in America. ("The 2015 Pulitzer Prize Winner in Investigative Reporting", 2015)He won his second Pulitzer in 2015 for investigative reporting for a story on Medicare which exposed a system which had cost taxpayers millions of dollars and forced the US government to release Medicare data for the first time in history.

It was during this second story that Carreyrou had got in touch with Clapper for assistance in understanding certain medical billing codes. The two men had struck up a professional relationship since then. Carreyrou wasn't aware of Theranos and his first pit stop was the weekend interview his own paper had published of Holmes and the *New Yorker* article.

Holmes' statements struck him as being like something a grade school student would utter, and given the accusations of Fuisz, via Clapper, it seemed as if there was a real story there. He began by getting in touch with Fuisz's group and later managed to contact Alan Beam, who was, at this point, the only person who had any sort of evidence against Theranos (Carreyrou, 2019).

Beam put him in touch with a number of his former colleagues but no one was willing to go on the record thanks to every one of them having received threats, when they had left Theranos, of retribution in case they broke confidentiality agreements. Beam had, meanwhile, received the eighteen emails from the Washington law firm and this proved a major boost to Carreyrou's investigation.

Meanwhile, Carreyrou noticed someone had viewed his LinkedIn profile. Someone who used to work at Theranos, named Tyler Shultz.

Pressure Tactics

It had been close to seven months since Shultz had quit Theranos and his grandfather had yet to believe a word of what his grandson was telling him. At a recent thanksgiving dinner, Tyler was forced to sit at a table and listen to Holmes preach about her love for the Shultz family. It was as if the old man had forgotten the threats Holmes had made against Tyler.

Carreyrou soon got in touch with him and they agreed to meet. Tyler was extra cautious, knowing Holmes' vindictive streak and used both a burner cell phone and a fake email account to communicate. They met at a beer garden in Palo Alto and Carreyrou was able to gather further information about the inside events at Theranos.

The very next day, as Shultz pulled into his parent's driveway, his father confronted him, asking whether he had been speaking to a reporter. George Shultz had just got off the phone, informing them that if Tyler valued his future he would stop talking to reporters and would meet the company's lawyers the next day.

Tyler called his grandfather and asked to meet him alone later that night, without any lawyers present. The elder Shultz agreed and Tyler visited his grandfather and once again, tried to tell him his side of the story. Shultz was still completely closed to listen to anything against Holmes and then told Tyler that there were lawyers waiting upstairs with documents for him to sign.

Tyler felt betrayed by this and saw it as his grandfather choosing Holmes' side once and for all. The lawyers from Boies Schiller tried to force Tyler into signing legal documents under the threat of a lawsuit, but he refused to sign anything. The elder Shultz seemed taken aback by the ferocity with which the lawyers were attacking his grandson, but it was too late to do anything about it (Carreyrou, 2019).

Eventually, Tyler refused to sign anything and refused to say anything until he hired a lawyer to defend himself. His grandfather was not happy and at this point, effectively cut him off, only communicating through Tyler's parents and lawyers, moving forward.

He hired a lawyer, Stephen Taylor, to defend him and soon negotiations between Boies Shiller and Taylor began. When they broke down, Boies resorted to the underhanded tactics they were famous for. Tyler's parents were threatened with bankruptcy and it was implied that all of them were under surveillance.

Since Tyler was barred from discussing details of the case with his parents, thanks to confidentiality agreements, he made sure his parents hired a lawyer as well so as to communicate through her. This new lawyer had her car broken into and her notes of the meeting were stolen.

Much like how Shultz was having the pressure applied to him, so were Erika Cheung and Alan Beam. Desperate to root out the source of the ongoing *WSJ* story, Boies stopped at nothing to threaten and intimidate the former employees of the company. After all, he had agreed to be paid in shares of the company instead of a fee. He was just protecting his investment, never mind the ethical lines he was crossing.

Investigation

The growing degree of pressure being applied to the ex-employees was thanks to Carreyrou's investigative efforts. After getting in touch with Shultz and Beam, he had felt it was time for Holmes to give him her side of the story and he contacted Theranos' PR representative. However, Holmes was perpetually busy and wasn't available for media appearances.

This was in direct contrast to her regular appearances on TV, be it 60 minutes or on a day time talk show, and Carreyrou soon found himself hosting a phalanx of lawyers from Boies Shiller. The lawyers tried intimidating Carreyrou and his editor (Carreyrou, 2019) but the *WSJ* was a far tougher proposition than a few ex-employees. Tails between their legs, the lawyers left.

Carreyrou, meanwhile, had been trying to track down doctors who were using Theranos' services for their patients. Arizona had been one of the first places Holmes had set up her operation in, and it was here he got in touch with Dr. Nicole Sundene who had ended up sending one of her patients to the emergency room thanks to Theranos' faulty test results.

Threats

In addition to Dr. Sundene, Carreyrou also got in touch with Dr. Adrienne Stewart. He provided samples of his blood to both doctors with a view to comparing Theranos' test results with those obtained from an established lab. Just as he expected, and as the doctors warned him, his results from Theranos were abnormal.

There were two scenarios which Alan Beam was worried about: One was a case where a faulty result would result in a patient seeking treatment for a condition they didn't have and the second, where a patient would not seek treatment for a condition they did have. The second case was far more serious since it could result in someone's death. By some miracle, this didn't happen.

Boies Shiller meanwhile got busy bullying the two doctors. Balwani took a hand as well, sending representatives to the doctors' clinics and forcing them to sign confidentiality agreements. Upon their refusal, Balwani threatened to drag their name through the mud and ruin their business.

Sure enough, Dr. Sundene began receiving inexplicably bad reviews on Yelp for her practice and she was forced to contact the company to have them deleted. Dr. Stewart was rattled further and she ultimately pleaded with Carreyrou to not use her name in any story the *WSJ* would print. (Carreyrou, 2019)

Holmes, meanwhile was busy palling around within the Obama administration, attending a state dinner for the Japanese prime minister and frequently photographed in political circles. She managed to lobby for and get a law passed that enabled residents of Arizona to have their blood tested without a doctor's orders. Also, Theranos' devices were cleared by the FDA to test for the virus HSV-1, a strain of herpes.

She was soon hosting the vice president, Joe Biden, at headquarters and he had his blood tested. She talked about getting emergency approval to have her devices shipped to Africa, where an Ebola epidemic was spreading. Then, in what was a truly genius attempt to kill the *WSJ* story, she went ahead and signed on a new investor.

The owner of the *WSJ*, Rupert Murdoch (Carreyrou, 2019).

Publication

Even as Carreyrou was busy putting the final touches on his expose, Holmes was busy trying to get Murdoch to quash the story. The *WSJ* had no idea all of this was going on and at one point, unbeknownst to Carreyrou, Holmes was in the same building as him, upstairs, trying to get Murdoch to do her bidding.

The billionaire refused to do so, however, and on October 15th 2015, an article titled "A Prized Startup's Struggles" blew the lid on all of Holmes' and Theranos' lies. Boies personally sent a number of letters to the newspaper, threatening all sorts of legal action, eventually escalating to a level where 23 pages (Carreyrou, 2019) were needed to fully do justice to all his threats.

The timing of the article was crucial. In just a few weeks, Holmes was due to appear at the *WSJ's* technology conference, the WSJ D.LIVE, and it was imperative that the paper get the story out before that. Holmes had refused to speak to Carreyrou all this while and this event would be an excellent opportunity for her to address the claims in the article.

For now, her response was to portray herself as a victim. Sighing that this is what happened to people who tried to change things, she vowed to clear her name. While playing the victim, she was preparing a final assault on the *WSJ*, but she received a huge blow before she could land a punch.

The FDA had just ruled that Theranos' nanotainers were an unapproved medical device. Holmes spun this story as a voluntary withdrawal on Theranos' part, but was unaware of a bigger problem on her hands. Late in September, an email had landed in the inbox of a veteran CMS inspector with the subject line "CMS Complaint:

Theranos Inc." (Carreyrou, 2019).

The person who had sent it was Erika Cheung.

Chapter 10: Fall From Grace

As the investigation had been gathering steam, the number of negative reviews of Theranos on Glassdoor, the workplace review website, began increasing. Balwani had always kept tabs on this and had instructed HR to counter the negative reviews with fake positive ones. He even went so far as to try to find employees who had written those reviews and as was his fashion, terrorized anyone who he thought was being disloyal.

Holmes, meanwhile, took the offensive in her first appearance after the article was published. The *WSJ* followed up with a second article about the nanotainers being withdrawn but she spun it as a voluntary choice. At the *WSJ* tech conference, she dismissed Carreyrou as "some guy who wrote stuff about us" (Carreyrou, 2019) and attacked the anonymity of his sources.

She claimed the ex-employees quoted were "confused" and that they hadn't worked at Theranos long enough to know what was going on. Lastly, she dismissed claims that Theranos had run finger prick samples on commercial machines, and that Theranos had the full blessing of regulators. All in all, it was a typical Holmes performance – full of bravado, but all lies and nothing substantial.

Further Violations

Silicon Valley's initial reaction to the story had been to dismiss it in a knee-jerk fashion. Marc Andreessen, the co-founder of Netscape and head of the venture capital firm Andreessen Horowitz, came to her defense. Andreessen's defense of Holmes didn't come just out of the purity of his heart. His wife had recently profiled Holmes as part of a feature in the *New York Times'* Style magazine.

As an aside, this was a prolific time for Andreessen's foot finding his mouth. An investor in Facebook, he would soon tweet his displeasure at the government of India rejecting Facebook's mobile internet venture on the grounds of net neutrality and as a form of digital colonialism. Andreessen tweeted that perhaps colonialism was good for India, given what the British did to it. Clearly, becoming a history expert was a side effect of creating a defunct internet browser.

When the story refused to go away though, the valley was forced to ask questions for the first time. Perhaps, just maybe, Holmes wasn't everything she claimed to be?

Strategy

Holmes' first move was to shuffle the aging former statesmen/yes men on her board to a side committee called the "Board of Counselors" and bring in her nuclear option, David Boies, as a board member. The *WSJ* promptly began receiving a flurry of communication from his law firm threatening litigation and the legal department at the paper knuckled down for a fight (Carreyrou, 2019).

Holmes began portraying the whole story as a misogynist's pipe dream. Reasoning that she was always described as "a young woman", Carreyrou was compensating for the fact that he couldn't stomach seeing a woman succeed (Carreyrou, 2019). She considered releasing a story disclosing that she had suffered from sexual assault while at Stanford. The truth of this claim is not known.

Channing Robertson, who had been receiving $500,000 per year to function as an adviser, dismissed claims against Theranos and compared Holmes to Newton, Mozart, and insert-your-own-genius (Carreyrou, 2019). Holmes, meanwhile, was awarded with the honor being *Glamour* magazine's Woman of the Year and used her acceptance speech to further underline the misogynist narrative (Carreyrou, 2019).

The hits from the *WSJ*, though, just kept coming. Walgreens was reportedly reconsidering its relationship with Theranos. Holmes had apparently tried to raise more money from investors right before the expose on the condition that none of the new investors sue the firm in the future. Safeway, finally and formally, pulled the plug on its long since dead deal with Theranos. The physician running the labs since Alan Beam's departure was completely unqualified to do so.

And then the big one in December 2015: CMS was reportedly inspecting Theranos' facilities after complaints from doctors and former employees' reports of fraud.

Inspections And The End

Erika Cheung's email to CMS was taken seriously enough by the agency to begin their inspection a few days later. Ironically, the same inspector who had visited Theranos during the LTC Shoemaker episode found himself inspecting the facility again. The company had moved to a new location since then, but the laboratory was still divided into two sections: One for the commercial analyzers and one containing the proprietary devices.

Balwani and lawyers from Boies Shiller met the inspectors in a conference room and tried their best to stall them and even refuse them access. Being federal regulators though, there was no refusing them and the inspectors stayed for four days, combing through all of Theranos' lab equipment and testing procedures.

Lab personnel were questioned, and to the inspectors, it seemed as if they had been coached to provide answers (Carreyrou, 2019). In late January, the agency released a letter indicating serious violations at Theranos' facilities saying that it posed "immediate jeopardy to patient health and safety" (Carreyrou, 2019). Theranos had ten days to come up with a correction plan or risk losing its federal license.

Theranos, however, put a spin on this, claiming that none of the infractions had anything to do with its proprietary devices and that it had already rectified most of the deficiencies CMS had found. This was an outright lie but there was no way to disprove it, thanks to the company hiding behind the trade secrets blanket.

Meanwhile, Holmes was busy cozying up to Chelsea and Hillary Clinton, who was at the time considered the leading candidate for the upcoming US presidential election. Pictures of Holmes speaking at a fundraiser along with the Clintons were a stark reminder of how politically connected Holmes was.

Carreyrou eventually developed a source within CMS who leaked the entire report to him and the results were far worse than anyone expected. It proved that Theranos had run the majority of its tests on commercial analyzers and that Holmes had lied about the usage of its proprietary devices. Furthermore, the Edisons were completely unreliable and their error rates were many multiples outside the acceptable range of error, making them completely unsafe for medical use.

The lab was also damned in the report. Theranos had allowed unqualified personnel to handle samples, had stored them improperly, stored expired reagents with valid ones etc., just as Dupuy had mentioned to Balwani a few years ago. A few days later the CMS sent a letter to Holmes threatening to ban her from the blood testing business for two years thanks to Theranos not rectifying the flaws the agency had found.

Once this report was published, Walgreens, astoundingly, gave Theranos thirty days to rectify its faults or else their agreement was to be terminated. On July 8th, 2016, the *WSJ* reported that Holmes was banned from any blood testing lab for a period of two years and Theranos' California facility had lost its accreditation.

Holmes professed deep regret for the turn events that had taken place and vowed to rectify things. Instead, it was Balwani who paid the price and took the fall for her. He was fired from the company and what's more, Holmes ended their relationship too. Theranos, in an effort to get back into compliance, voided over two year's worth of blood test results, admitting its analyzers were faulty. This shocked Walgreens and eventually, they would sue Theranos in November of that year to the tune of $140 million, thus shutting the door well after the horse had bolted.

Holmes and Balwani were now the subject of a criminal investigation from the U.S. attorney's office in San Francisco and the SEC was about to slap charges of fraud against them as well. Despite all of this, Holmes still had her share of supporters and fought back in the public eye.

At an academic conference in August, she touted the technology Theranos had created but when questioned by a panel of experts, her story fell apart and the consensus was that she had blown her last chance to recover some credibility. In November 2016, David Boies finally cut ties with Theranos and Holmes, ostensibly over a disagreement over how to handle the government investigations (Carreyrou, 2019).

Presumably, Holmes felt Boies wasn't threatening the families of government prosecutors enough? Either way, Boies wrote down his investment in the company and moved on, professing "no regrets" for the way his firm handled things and using it as evidence of what a great lawyer he is (Stewart, 2018).

Soon, in early 2017, the company's second lab in Arizona failed inspection as well and was shut down. Theranos paid close to $4.5 million to reimburse patients in Arizona for faulty blood tests. The number of blood tests that were voided was close to a million. As of this writing, a class action lawsuit is pending in the Arizona courts.

The Partner Fund sued Theranos to the tune of $43 million and won. Walgreens would settle its case for $25 million as well. By the end of 2017, Theranos had burned close to $900 million, most of it in legal fees but had secured funding from the private equity firm, Fortress Investment Group (Carreyrou, 2019).

Fortress' investment came with a number of conditions though. Theranos' patents were collateral for the investment and there were a number of operational milestones the company would have to hit in order to see the money. Theranos never did hit the milestones and the current status of the patents is unknown. Theranos did end up laying off most of its workforce though.

In the spring of 2018, Holmes and Balwani were finally charged by the SEC. That summer, Holmes and Balwani were indicted on nine counts of wire fraud and two counts of conspiracy to commit wire fraud by a grand jury. Holmes tried to pivot Theranos away from blood tests to, instead, becoming a manufacturer of blood testing machines for laboratories (Carreyrou, 2019).

It didn't work. In September 2018, Theranos was dissolved, making Holmes a brilliant Stanford dropout once again, with the title of fraud appended to her name. Investors who poured in over $900 million dollars lost all their money, with some recovering it through lawsuits and some still seeking damages.

Both Holmes and Balwani maintain their innocence.

Current Whereabouts

Holmes and Balwani are currently fighting the case against them in court. The case has still not gone to trial and their defense is apparently resting on proving that the government regulators acted improperly by responding to Carreyrou's tips. By doing so, they were clearly acting under the influence of an outsider whose aim it was to malign Holmes and Theranos (Henning, 2019).

This is being viewed as a high risk/high reward strategy. If it comes off, Holmes will avoid jail time. If it doesn't, she will face jail time. Either way, given the multitude of documents that need to be reviewed, a trial date is far off. Holmes, now 35, has settled her case with the SEC, paying a fine of $500,000 and accepting her ban from holding top positions in any company for ten years.

Meanwhile, reportedly, she has found love with the heir of a wealthy San Diego based family who own a chain of hotels. Reportedly, the couple are engaged and the *New York Post* reports of rifts within her fiancé's family (Schuster, 2019).

Given the description of Billy Evans, her fiancé, as a former playboy who was the "bad cop" to the CEO's good cop at his former place of employment, his attempts at a poorly conceived startup previously, and accounts from his friends of his ability to manipulate people, it seems as if Holmes has found a replica of Balwani, sans the getting-lucky-before-the-dot-com bust part.

Either way, Holmes is now mentioned as a cautionary tale for investors and is a frequent subject of legal sections of newspapers and April Fool's day articles of President Trump anointing her the next head of the FDA ("Trump Taps Elizabeth Holmes to Lead FDA - SynBioBeta", 2018). Given the current state of governmental affairs, in what is either a compliment or a rebuke, Holmes has been christened a bigger liar than "even Donald Trump" (Zahm, 2019).

Not everyone in this story is lucky enough to be compared to the incomparable President of the United States, however. Some have actually moved on with their lives.

Tyler Shultz is now the CEO and co-founder of a company, Flux Biosciences. The company aims to conduct in-vitro diagnostics using blood, urine and sweat samples and correlate it to data obtained from activity trackers ("Flux Biosciences", 2019). He has mended fences with his grandfather, George Shultz, as per a statement the older man issued to ABC's *Nightline*. Shultz stated he was proud of his grandson's actions and praised his courage and integrity in the face of threats and intimidation (Dunn, 2018).

Erika Cheung has set up a non-profit of her own, named Ethics in Entrepreneurship, which aims to educate college graduates of the ethical challenges they will face either running their own companies or working for one. Unlike Tyler Shultz, no one in Erika's family discouraged her from blowing the whistle on Theranos' practices and supported her fully (Jagannathan, 2019).

Billion Dollar Facade

Richard Fuisz, who somehow found himself a hero in all of this, divorced his wife who was good friends with Noel Holmes, though not for that cause. Perhaps miffed at the lack of publicity he subsequently received, he did grant a few interviews around the time Carreyrou's book, *Bad Blood*, was released. In an interview, Fuisz blamed Holmes' parents for indulging her childish fantasies to become an inventor, "like Dr. Fuisz" (Cohan, 2018).

Rochelle Gibbons continues to place full blame on Holmes and Boies' intimidation tactics for the death of her husband Ian. She believes the choice they gave him to either perjure himself or lose his job broke Ian. She characterizes Holmes as a "pathological liar" and as someone who "should be in jail and not be allowed to destroy people's lives" (Dunn, 2018).

John Carreyrou, to whom this book owes a lot, continues to report on the case against Holmes and Theranos. Holmes' legal team is doing their absolute best to avoid having him testify against her, knowing that if he does so, a conviction is almost certain.

What of all the investors Holmes duped? Well, a lot of them are understandably cagey about the whole affair. One man who isn't is one of the first investors in Theranos, Tim Draper. At a Bloomberg event on March 8th 2019, Draper affirmed he would back Holmes as a "chief scientific officer but not a CEO" (Diop, 2019).

Rupert Murdoch sold his shares back to Holmes for the paltry price of $1, thereby taking a loss of over $100 million. However, he offset this against his other gains and thereby could reduce the amount of taxes he owed, making his the best case scenario in all of this.

Meanwhile, former senior level employees of Theranos have reportedly struggled to find employment elsewhere. Given the insular world of Silicon Valley, most of their searches have been concentrated in the same area. The only person who seems to have managed an escape is the former Chiat\Day executive, Patrick O'Neill, who had eventually joined Theranos as creative director (Carreyrou, 2019).

Of the H-1B employees, understandably, nothing is known. It is questionable whether anyone, be it Theranos or the legal system in general, ever cared for their well-being.

Chapter 11: Seeds Of A Fraud

The Theranos saga shows how, under the right circumstances and with the right sort of person, virtually anyone can be hoodwinked. There are a number of lessons one can take from all of this, not least investors and other prospective founders of companies. Mind you, not all of the available lessons are positive.

For one, it is borderline terrifying how easily Holmes was able to subvert all opposition to her and how easily she managed to charm the number of people she did. It's not as if these people are unintelligent either. George Shultz built his career negotiating deals as the secretary of state during the height of the Cold War. As skilled a negotiator as he was, he failed to see through Holmes' lies.

Holmes remains an extremely skilled manipulator of people and is no doubt as ruthless about what she wants as before. Even at this point, she has the audacity to seek funding for another idea she claims she has. The existence of people like Tim Draper shows that she will not lack support when and if she puts her legal troubles behind her.

It is instructive to understand the environment which enabled Holmes to play out her hoax. For all the deserved vitriol Wall Street receives for its role in the economy, perhaps we need to take pause and consider that a greater source of danger is being ignored. For all the good that Silicon Valley has done, it remains an easy prey to the sort of traps that Wall Street has long since fallen into.

We will need to step back in time here, but please bear with this. It'll be a worthwhile journey which will help explain the Theranos mess in more detail.

Roots

On July 5th 1994, Amazon.com was founded in Bellevue, Washington by Jeff Bezos. The new company was an online book retailer but this didn't even begin to cover the vision Bezos had for his new venture.

Ultimately, the snowball that Bezos began would morph into something that even he, perhaps, hadn't envisioned.

The Problem

Silicon Valley had existed long before Bezos, of course. Always the home of brainy computer types, since the days of Ham radio, Intel, Xerox, HP and later Apple and Microsoft, the valley has produced its fair share of geniuses and game changers. In the early eighties, Larry Ellison and Oracle changed the face of B2B software just as Bill Gates and Steve Jobs changed the meaning of the word "computer".

However, there's a reason we need to start with Bezos. Unlike his predecessors, Bezos didn't come from a purely computing background (neither did Jobs but Jobs tends to defy all convention).He attended Princeton and studied electrical engineering and computer science. He graduated Princeton at a curious time in Wall Street's history.

The Street is and always has been about making money. It has never promised to change the world or try to do some greater good. This is actually a good thing because when dealing with your average Wall Street firm and examining its actions, one always knows where they stand. By the late '80s, trading software was taking over the Street and its misuse had already caused a crash in 1988, termed "Black Monday".

There was no doubt, though, that computers and algorithms were the future. Completely immune to emotional decisions and less likely to execute simple fat finger mistakes, computerized trading programs and networks were something Wall Street firms began investing in as early as the mid 80s.

Thus, brilliant young graduates like Bezos were in high demand. His first job out of college was to build a network for international trade facilitation at Fitel, a fintech company which existed before the word Fintech itself did. From there, Bezos graduated to working for banks and finally, a hedge fund.

Wall Street remains a curious mix of traders and investors. The traders are interested mostly in modeling the markets and figuring out short term patterns. Investors are, supposedly, more interested in the fundamentals of a business and its long term prospects. Earnings projections and a company's ability to meet them are of paramount importance.

Bill Gates figured this out early, thanks to his intelligence and partly due to his friendship with Warren Buffett. Microsoft's earnings per share under Gates were always around a cent or two cents greater than Wall Street analyst projections and thus, earning the tag of "over-performer", Microsoft was able to grow its market capitalization (which is its share price multiplied by the total number of shares) by leaps and bounds.

This led to Gates and his partners becoming ultra rich. While Steve

Jobs, his one-time rival, didn't play the earnings game, he nonetheless played Wall Street's game in other ways. Ensuring huge product launches, creating a cult-like customer base through marketing and ensuring Apple products were the all-round best looking, are all hallmarks of what analysts tend to look for in a company.

The fact remains that the iPod was a clunky piece of hardware to use, even by the standards of the early 2000s, relying entirely on integrating with iTunes and having a complicated process of uploading media to it, unlike other media devices at the time. However, it was Apple that received the accolades, and through the self-validating circle of Wall Street hype, the likes of Creative and Sony were banished from the marketplace simply because public perception of them as being "innovative" had eroded.

Thus, we can reduce Wall Street's expectations of companies to two things: Earnings and products. This is a huge oversimplification, of course, but it serves the purposes of our story. This is where Bezos faced a problem. Amazon as a startup neither had the earnings nor did it have any products since it was an online retailer and merely sold other people's products. By any estimate then, his company was doomed to obscurity.

Bezos was not the first entrepreneur to try his hand at selling things on the internet. The internet shopping network and Netmarket preceded him. These never really took off the ground and were mostly hobby projects. Bezos was different from the creators of these sites. You see, he had inside information from his Wall Street experience.

Cash Flow

Bezos' Wall Street jaunt had occurred due to its growing technological demands. While the Street benefited from Bezos, Bezos gained much, much more in return. He realized that the key to Amazon's growth was to get the analysts to focus on something other than earnings, given that Amazon would have none.

More importantly, in the light of what Amazon has since become, it's clear that Bezos had no intention of producing earnings for a long, long time. Analysts' reliance on earnings has sound reasoning behind it. After all, if a business doesn't make money, how can it survive?

Bezos turned this argument on its head. As far as he saw, if a business had the ability to meet its costs and constantly raise cash for its future expenses and investments, why would it need to make money? Well, the business would certainly survive but the owners wouldn't become rich. After all if everything you're earning is being eaten up by investment back into the business, your wealth as an owner remains stagnant.

However, if Amazon was a public company, Bezos' net worth would depend on its stock market valuation, not its earnings. There is a key difference here. While stock market valuations up to that point have depended on earnings, the two of them are not the same. Stock market valuations depended on what the public thought the business was worth. They used the earnings to determine this worth.

If Bezos could convince people to look at something other than earnings, he could ensure Amazon's valuation would grow as a company. So what did Amazon have in abundance? Why, cash flow, of course! Given that Amazon was constantly plunging cash into its businesses, always reinvesting and always growing thus causing a greater need as years passed for more and more cash, its cash flow was always going to be high.

Thus, Bezos convinced analysts that as long as Amazon's cash flow needs were met, the business would run perpetually. The analysts bought this argument and helped change the perception of the stock which rose in value. As the value of the stock rose, more people bought into the argument and were willing to give Bezos even more cash to grow and meet his reinvestment needs.

This is the real genius of Jeff Bezos and it is something that is not recognized enough, given his other achievements. He might not have realized it at the time but by discrediting earnings for business valuation, he had turned the very concept of a business on its head.

Thus, a business no longer needed to make money in order to be considered successful. With the right cocktail of a genius founder, willing investors and the right marketing, a business can have genuine value even though the factors going into it sound completely insubstantial and made up.

Amazon, to this day, has a poor record when it comes to free cash flow metrics. Free cash flow is the amount of remaining cash a company has after it has reinvested everything back into its business (Kenton, 2019). Given its size these days, this metric is a lot better but for the first decade and more of its existence, Amazon threw up zero cash for its investors. It didn't matter, though, since the stock price kept going up all the while.

Whatever you might think of all this, Amazon has always managed to have almost no competitors by virtue of it being the first company to crack this cash flow code with Wall Street. Ebay, the company it is usually lumped together with, is a very different company in that it offers a clear value proposition, which is an online auction. Amazon has never offered this and thus, does not belong in the same category.

In the following decade, a further incendiary ingredient would be added to this mix. It would happen thanks to Mark Zuckerberg and his shenanigans with FaceMash.

Prankster To CEO

Zuckerberg taught himself to code on his parents computer when he was eleven years old (Carreyrou, 2019). A prodigy much in the vein of Bill Gates and Steve Wozniak, he was and always will be a prodigious technical talent. What is more questionable, though, is his business chops. This is a ridiculous thing to say about the founder of a $533.76 billion company, but let's travel back to the early 2000's when the seed was planted.

It is a fact that Zuckerberg, for all his talents, never did create a unique product. FaceMash, the project that got him into hot water, was essentially a localized Harvard version of HotorNot, which was launched in 2000. Even Facebook, or "The Facebook" as it was initially called, was not a unique idea.

Social networks had been around for a while by that point, prime examples being MySpace, Google's Orkut and Friendster. So what differentiated Facebook from all of these other products? There have been many explanations over the years but ultimately, it all came down to one thing: Virality.

The word didn't exist at the time, but through some social cocktail, Zuckerberg's product managed to engage its users, which in turn fed user growth and on and on until its growth was beyond exponential.

Bezos' business strategy was paying dividends beyond Amazon. The earliest profiteers of this were the pioneers of the digital age who, flush with their millions, began funding businesses which had models similar to their own. Google was one of the first to profit from this. After all, at the time, the founders of Google had no idea how they would monetize their search engine.

Similarly, YouTube when it started was simply a social video sharing platform with no aim of monetization. What enabled these companies to grow were the funds that were pouring in from investors who, themselves, had gotten rich creating businesses that didn't need to make money. All they were looking for was an edge which would enable the product to retain users. In short, they were looking for viral potential.

Facebook was the first truly viral growth story. A product that was not unique - Google and YouTube had at least this justification - it had nothing going for it beyond the fact that people wanted to sign up to it. This convinced the newly rich venture capital investors of Silicon Valley that it was worth a punt and the millions then poured in.

While traditional investors were circumspect towards this new business model, the new venture capitalists showed how wealth could be created out of thin air. This wealth building model, from an investor's and a founder's perspective, deserves a deeper look.

Value Versus Valuation

How did a traditional business generate wealth for its owners? Well, it generated profits which gave the owners earnings for which they could pay themselves. The higher the profits, the more they could pay themselves. In short, the business generated value via profits.

Amazon and later to a much greater degree, Facebook, upended all of that. During Facebook's private company phase, there were no profits to speak of. In fact, Zuckerberg actively opposed monetizing the platform, as detailed in the account of Eduardo Saverin (Mezrich, 2009), his one time partner in the company. So why were investors queuing up to give him their money?

Well, to begin with, he had users. The fact that the users were present was enough to convince the new venture capitalists that, with enough users captured, at some point, even a small fee would result in a massive profit. Think of it this way: If five billion people collectively agree to use your product and are willing to pay one dollar per year to use it, you've earned five billion in revenue.

The key factor was the rate of user growth, more explosive the better. Facebook had this and the initial investors were in. Given the increasing number of users, which were the mark of its valuation, subsequent investors had to pay higher prices to join the club. For example if the first investor paid $2 per share on the basis of Facebook having 100 users, the next investor would $4 per share for FB having 400 users and so on.

Thus, the first investor has seen their investment double from $2 per share to $4 per share. Put another way, if they invested $10 million, it turned into $20 million during the next round of funding. Now imagine 5 rounds of funding followed by an IPO, which is when a private company goes public. IPOs always result in a massive increase in valuation.

Seeing that the first few investors have doubled their investment, due to the fear of missing out on overnight riches, subsequent investors clamber over each other to get on board, no matter how ridiculous the product is. This is what gave Zuckerberg the power to attend investment meetings in his pyjamas and be lauded for his audacity, instead of being chucked out on his ear (Mezrich, 2009).

Thus, in this world, the ultimate money maker for an investor was not the value or profits a business generated, but its valuation. What will someone in the future pay for this business? That's essentially what valuation is. This is what enabled Peter Thiel, an initial investor of Facebook, to turn his $100 million-odd investment into over a billion dollars once FB went public.

Does this make him an investment genius? The word is out on that. Given that he founded PayPal with Elon Musk, Thiel certainly has tech chops and is not a lightweight. However, there's no denying that this valuation game gives charlatans like Ramesh Balwani access to instant riches and the subsequent influence it brings.

Balwani got rich playing the valuation game. What was CommerceBid's value? Nothing. It went bankrupt along with its buyer, Commerce One. However, Balwani got rich because he received a high valuation for his business from a greater fool at the time.

Investment Genius

The valuation game is not without risk. There's no way anyone can guarantee or predict virality. After all, what makes Gangnam Style better than any other random K-pop video? No one knows. People just know when they see it. Why did the Harlem Shake take off as it did? Why do social media challenges go viral? No one knows in advance.

In the business world, this had huge ramifications from an investment standpoint. What makes WhatsApp a superior product to Skype? For all intents and purposes, Skype was a better bet. It had better video calling integrated into it and arrived as a mobile app earlier. However, it is WhatsApp that dominates the mobile space.

Forget Skype, what makes WhatsApp better than Viber or WeChat or any of the other messaging apps? Aside from the number of users, nothing. Photo filtering was not an original idea by any means but what made Instagram so famous? We just don't know. It is no coincidence that Facebook purchased both these apps. To this day, Instagram doesn't make a profit and WhatsApp isn't even monetized but it doesn't matter.

Not buying it would have been a bigger mistake. So here we have a quandary, from an investor's standpoint: Missing out can cause very real problems but the key issue of which product generates higher valuation is something extremely nebulous. How does one manage the risk?

Simple, an investor diversifies. Therefore, when a venture capital firm invests in a startup, they invest their money in tens of other similar startups. For every Uber that gets invested in, Lyft, Careem, Ola and other clones receive equal investment. This way, an investor's money is not concentrated into one basket, but spread out.

If the business potential or edge the startup has is huge, such as being first with an innovative solution like Google was, or an extremely smart founder with viral potential, like Zuckerberg and Facebook were, then the need to diversify is less.

If the startup is a clone of another successful company, the need to diversify is less as well. Since the business model has been proven successful, there's greater assurance that the new venture will succeed. Examples of such investors are Germany's Rocket Ventures limited, run by the Samwer brothers, who invest only in clones.

Thus, one of the Indian Amazon clones they invested in, named Jabong.com, eventually got swallowed up by a bigger competitor and now doesn't exist. The company never made any profits during its time but none of that mattered. The Samwers played the valuation game and got rich when the company was bought out.

Google routinely buys out smaller algorithm developers. By doing so, they're not only buying out potential future competitors but also looking to integrate the next viral feature into their own platform. Out of the ten that they invest in, they lose money with nine of them. However, that one investment more than pays off for the remaining nine, and this is how investors generate money.

Venture capital firms such as Andreessen Horowitz and Lucas Ventures make money in this manner. Thus, there's no great business genius here beyond playing the odds well. Yes, it does take skill to line up basic factors but experience in the industry more than provides this to an investor.

Even start up incubators, such as Y Combinator, require qualifying startups to have exponential user growth. It doesn't matter if you're curing cancer or if you're sculpting menhirs; as long as you have exponential user growth, you can stay and attract funding and grow to bigger valuations. You will need to make money someday but worry about that once you have a billion engaged users.

Thus, Jeff Bezos' initial idea to have Wall Street value his cash flow instead of his earnings had grown into a Frankenstein's monster of everyone chasing each other, worried about missing out on the next big thing.

Billion Dollar Facade

Into all of this, stepped Elizabeth Holmes.

Chapter 12: A Perfect Storm

Silicon Valley had and has other problems beyond the playing of the valuation game instead of creating business value. Given the technical nature of the work involved and society's insistence of pushing boys instead of girls towards technical fields, there is a notable imbalance between genders in the workplace.

Going back to its roots, the valley has rarely seen any female founders of note. The most famous and respected current female personalities happen to hold executive leadership positions within the bigger firms, like Sheryl Sandberg at Facebook and Marissa Meyer at Yahoo.

There has not been a female Gates, Ellison, Zuckerberg or Thiel. It is a bit astonishing that mediocrity amongst male tech founders is rarely punished but finding a single female founder is harder than looking for ice in a desert.

In this regard, Silicon Valley is very much like Wall Street. There is a real issue when it comes to gate keeping with regards to women in tech, which is evident with the occasional scandals that erupt. #Gamergate morphed from a domestic dispute involving a male developer being dumped by his female developer girlfriend into a referendum on which sex was superior.

While the protagonists of that scandal were hardly innocent themselves, the amount of vitriol which was directed towards the woman in question and the equally fundamentalist reaction from feminist voices shows that technology as a sector, not just Silicon

Valley, has failed thus far to handle this issue in a balanced manner.

The events which led to the resignation of Uber's founder, Travis Kalanick, as CEO, show both the challenges women face in such workplaces, as well as the fact that times are changing for the better. Thus, when Elizabeth Holmes popped up on the scene, Silicon Valley and the tech world in general was hungry for an ambitious and visionary woman to take the lead and show the way.

Then, there was also the disruption mania that gripped the valley.

Change

The rate at which the world has been changing since 1995 is completely unprecedented in human history. What would have once taken hundreds of years to play out has instead happened in half a lifetime. People who were born in the late 1980s have gone from a world where cell phones didn't exist to one where they don't need to exist anymore. Smartphones contain computers that are more powerful than the computer which put human beings on the moon.

Naturally, technology has changed the way we do many things. It has caused multiple industries to become obsolete and forced others to overhaul their way of working in order to survive. Newspapers are a prime example of this. These days, if you wish to catch up on what happened around the world while you were asleep, Twitter is a far better source than the *New York Times*, despite Twitter not employing a single journalist.

Humans are notoriously bad at dealing with change. Right from childhood, we're conditioned to love stability (Goldberg & Carlson,

2014). Given the rate at which things are changing, though, we haven't been able to keep up and develop a healthy relationship with everything happening. Thus, what has resulted is a Wild West sort of scenario where anyone can voice their opinion, no matter how uninformed, and a troll ends up being elected President.

Learning

Valley firms have had firsthand experience dealing with all this change. When Facebook and Google started out, data was a nebulous thing. All Google wanted to do was to help you find stuff on the web. These days, data security is even more important that money, with one leak having the power to change your life.

These firms have had to navigate unexplored paths when it comes to all of this. Mark Zuckerberg had to go from mocking people who posted their phone numbers on The Facebook to sitting in front of a Congressional Committee a decade and a half later, explaining how his firm's data security apparatus is greater than that of the Pentagon's.

Thus, when a firm sets out with the noble aim of changing the way something is done, it is entering unknown waters. Witness the trouble Uber has had around the world dealing with unionized taxi services. There is no doubt that Uber's vision, from taxi services to food delivery to mass transit, is one which will eliminate all sorts of problems for consumers.

However, consider the implications and the accompanying legislation Uber needs to subject itself to. Take the mass transit ambitions of the company. If this vision is realized, both public transport and the motor vehicle industry will become obsolete. Cars will go the way of horses, with only pleasure vehicles, such as Ferraris and other high end sports cars, being in demand.

An average automaker in this scenario, like Ford or BMW, becomes just a hardware provider who builds the outer body of the vehicle. Google, Apple and Uber provide the software which powers the cars. This vision is so mind-bending that most of us cannot compute such a world.

While the maturation of this vision sees Uber becoming a mass vehicle manufacturer or car company, what happens while it navigates the path to that vision? It is inherently a tech company and works within the norms and practices which govern that industry. The norms for a tech company and those governing a vehicle manufacturer are completely different, in terms of workplace culture, goals, industry economics and regulation.

Is Uber capable of navigating both worlds at once? Can it be a high tech company and be a lower tech, boring, car company at the same time? This is the real challenge disruption poses and is one that Silicon Valley is asking itself only now. To be fair, this is not something any human can envision in advance perfectly. The truth is, most of these companies are learning as they go, much like the rest of us.

Then there's the question of legislation. Legislation simply doesn't exist to govern such companies so the only thing governing them is ethics. Ethics is something which varies by industry as well, since different industries have different human consequences. Bill Gates sending out low quality versions of Windows was hardly as big a catastrophe as a food manufacturer shipping out baby formula that failed quality checks.

Gates never had to straddle worlds but his successors in the valley had to. Given the lack of legislation and any guiding foresight, it seems natural that a lot of companies fell back on the only guidance that was available to them: Their existing industry's guidelines.

Methods

"Move fast, break things." This is one of Zuckerberg's most famous quotes and is a motto Facebook lives by. Zuckerberg figured this out when he pivoted Facebook almost overnight from being a desktop oriented dinosaur to a mobile-centric app after the iPhone was released.

He didn't know what the mobile landscape was going to be like and the only way he could find out was to go full steam ahead and make mistakes. If he didn't, Facebook would have become obsolete within a few years. This is an approach that all tech firms take and it remains the best way to work when dealing with applications.

However, it doesn't work when your product crosses over to multiple industries. Uber tried to move fast and break things but all that it did was get it embroiled in lawsuits. In large parts of the world, Uber is now simply a regular taxi service as a result, on par with traditional services, and a far cry from the ride sharing, open-economy driver Kalanick envisioned it as.

Zuckerberg's philosophy also suggests taking a lax view of the existing rules. After all, the rules don't really exist at the frontier and you need to make them up yourself. However, in an established industry, rules exist for a very good reason and this approach doesn't work, as Zuckerberg himself is finding out.

The only way to progress, then, is to adopt the traditional work methods of established companies within the space. Thus, Uber has to adopt the work practices of a regular taxicab operator and this is not a very enticing view of things, understandably, for a high tech firm. What is the point of being high tech and trying to change things if you're going to do exactly the same thing at the end of the day?

Holmes And Theranos

This chapter-and-a-half-long digression finally arrives at its point. The unique cocktail of valuation, lack of a female founder and a "move fast, break things" motto, led to the toxic rise of Theranos and explains why so many otherwise intelligent people seemingly looked the other way.

For one thing, Holmes ticked a lot of the right boxes. She was a young woman, obviously very smart, and she had a huge vision which Steve Jobs would have been proud of. Her investors did not need to make money since all they cared about was the valuation of the business. Thus, all she needed to do was to provide great projections instead of actual revenue or profit.

Her role as a CEO was to make sure her company received as high a valuation as possible. In such a role, cutting costs in the short run to boost profit would have been detrimental. Thus, we have the perverse situation where a CEO is doing a bad job because her company is making money.

Lastly, in order to innovate, Theranos had to break the rules. The key point here being: The rules that governed traditional blood analysis methods, not the regulatory framework within which the practice exists. It is telling that not a single one of Holmes' investors came from a medical device background.

Silicon Valley has a number of VC firms which operate in the medical technology space and given that not a single one of them felt Holmes' plan was workable, other investors should have taken note. However, as we've seen, none of them did and some still continue to turn a blind eye.

Why Did Holmes Do It?

When seen through the prism of "move fast, break things", Holmes decision to press ahead and secure business despite having malfunctioning analyzers is easy to understand. She was not doing anything wrong or even unethical if she truly believed that her team would get the analyzers right at some point before being deployed in stores.

Her mistake, among the many she made, was to forget that her analyzers were not an app on a phone but machines which had very real human consequences. Beyond a certain point, it became imperative to stop and actually make sure they worked before pressing ahead.

However, she would have failed at her job as a CEO if she did so. Stopping the solicitation of customers would have been akin to stopping the hunt for more users. If a company stops growing its user base at an exponential rate, investors lose interest and pull their funds. If their funds are pulled, where was Theranos to get the money to develop its analyzers?

This vicious circle is something a lot of startup CEOs find

themselves in and most of them do not make it out, understandably. This is why the tech scene is dominated by the few who did make it out: The likes of Facebook, Apple, Microsoft, and Google. This is also why a lot of startups prefer to sell to a larger company instead of going at it alone.

By becoming a division of a larger company, the former CEO receives breathing room within which he or she can refine their product. The larger balance sheet provides a good buffer against tough times which a startup can otherwise never hope to weather.

Holmes' problem in this regard was that there was no ideal company out there which could take over Theranos and bail her out. Quest labs and the like were well established players but from the "old" industry side of the tracks. She would never have fit into such cultures, even if she was sincere about her desire for change and not a fraud.

Given her upbringing and unquestionable intelligence, it is more than plausible that Holmes genuinely believed she would change the world with her devices. Somewhere along the way though, she crossed that line of no return, roughly around the time when she was courting Walgreens, and realized that there was no going back now. Her ego simply wouldn't allow it.

Allied to this was the fact that she was becoming richer and richer on paper, thanks to the valuations Theranos was receiving, which was extremely important to her. Lastly, the influence of someone like Balwani could hardly have been positive. She has never spoken in an honest fashion about those days, so all we can ask is, surely, she must have known that it would all fall apart one day?

Her fame and wealth grew but Theranos' devices never moved beyond their initial prototype stage which was way back in 2005.

Surely, as an intelligent and aware person, she should have seen it all coming? At the height of her fame, did she know it was all going to come crashing down soon, simply because all of it was unsustainable?

We don't know for now. Perhaps Holmes' lies overtook her to the extent that she began to believe her own utterances. She wasn't the first to do so and will not be the last.

The Future For Medical Device Innovation

Genalyte's unofficial tagline is "Like Theranos, but it works" (Raphael, 2019). It is a good summation of what their device is all about. While there aren't any claims of requiring just a few drops of blood, Genalyte does require less amounts of blood than usual medical tests. The CEO of the company, Cary Gunn, has had to deal with a lot of press about Holmes as one can imagine.

Ironically, one person whose company is also caught up in Holmes' mess is Tyler Shultz. While people are perfectly happy to celebrate his role as a whistle-blower in the Theranos saga, his appearances at medical technology conferences are often met with questions about the veracity of his claims as to his device's efficacy. Life is nothing if not ironic.

While the FDA and CMS are working to close regulatory loopholes that Theranos exploited, the fact remains that the future for wearable medical device research is an area where regulation has to be developed as we go along. Holmes inadvertently let the regulators know how much they were missing and even scarier, how much they don't know.

One can think of this field as producing controversies of the same kind when Google released its Glass. There simply wasn't any sort of legal framework that could handle such a device, be it from a privacy or a safety standpoint. Saying "I don't know" is something people don't respond well to and the authorities, thus, are not saying this despite it being the truth.

For now, a future full of wearable health monitoring and diagnostic devices seems inevitable. Activity trackers are already all the rage among fitness enthusiasts and even laypersons are aware of the 10,000 steps in a day rule for fitness that step counters on phones have popularized.

It seems logical to add a diagnostic element to these devices given the data they collect. The data poses another challenge: Back when Holmes was conceiving her vision of Theranos devices existing in homes, data was not a concern since we didn't know anything about it.

Now, though, every company needs to devote as much attention to data security as it does to innovation. The next few years will see a wave of legislation with regards to home assistants, like Google Home, Amazon's Alexa, Apple's Siri etc. The amount of information such devices collect are often ignored thanks to the cover that smart aleck responses provide, especially in Siri's case.

Extended to the medical field, how ethical is it that a company like Genalyte will have access to parts of your medical history, as it must, in order to diagnose conditions? How much of your data will your doctor have to share with this private firm? If you agree to share the data in order for the company to build a disease map, like Holmes envisioned, could that data be misused by a rogue agent to determine which disease that population is the most susceptible to?

Could a rogue state with advanced technical abilities hack such data and initiate biological warfare? The events unfolding in Ukraine have already shown how a ruthless, more technically advanced actor can subjugate and wreak havoc on another. Cyber warfare between the major powers of the world is an almost daily occurrence. With the physical arms race, eventually, all actors progressed to biological warfare. Is it unreasonable to expect the same to occur in the cyberspace, once enough data is collected via devices?

One of the side effects of the technological advances we've made is that, any mistake which is made within the tech space leads to far larger consequences than anything else in the past. If a solar storm, which is uncontrollable as an event, were to knock out communications on Earth today, the number of deaths it would cause would dwarf the worst genocide we can think of (Byrd, 2019).

This not because of solar storms being harmful to us physically, but its effects on the technology we use. Imagine, planes literally dropping out of the sky and such. Who knows what other hidden dangers lie? In the words of that other great visionary who once lied to the world like Holmes did, "There are too many unknown unknowns".

Conclusion

Elizabeth Holmes is still battling in the courts and sticks to her vision doggedly. In her mind, as far as her public utterances go, she hasn't done anything wrong. At the time of Carreyrou's expose, Theranos was about to expand into California and it is safe to say that the *WSJ* article saved lives.

It has become fashionable these days to label anything one doesn't agree with as "fake news". This whole affair, however, proves the importance of a free and fair press. The biggest hero in all of this is John Carreyrou, and deservedly so.

The ethics with which Silicon Valley governs itself came under close scrutiny thanks to this case and it bears remembering that the most successful tech CEOs have been so since their days in college. Viewed from a human standpoint, they have been forced to grow up in the public eye and they largely seem to be maturing as they grow older, just like humans do.

Thus, while it is easy to wave our hands and blame this whole mess on toxic work cultures and such, the truth is that this work culture has produced more innovation than at any other point in human history. A lot of the conveniences we take for granted have happened due to the vision and work ethic of such people.

Are they to blame for one woman who perverted what they stood for? Should they take equal blame as the Theranos board members who refused to do their job and rein in their out of control, megalomaniac CEO? The answer is obvious really.

Thanks to diversifying their investments, it's unlikely the VC funds lost a lot of money, from an overall portfolio perspective. Those who did lose a lot of money were probably the former statesmen on the board, given their lack of investment experience. However, the thought that such people need money is laughable.

Furthermore, the idea that people like George Shultz, Henry Kissinger or "Mad Dog" Mattis will stand in front of a jury and receive penalties for their gross negligence of board duties is something that's not even worth discussing. Given the power they command, they've surely pardoned themselves a while back.

So what's the lesson in all of this? Well, there is some lesson for sure. Some people have contrasted Holmes with Jobs and mentioned why she was nothing like him. Indeed, Steve Jobs was not a fraud, so mentioning anything else seems moot.

Let's just say, we'll find out what the real lessons are as we go along. Much like a lot of the consequences of disruption, we simply don't know at this point.

Phil C. Senior

Connect with us on our Facebook page

www.facebook.com/bluesourceandfriends and stay tuned to our

latest book promotions and free giveaways.

Bibliography

Byrd, D. (2019). Are solar storms dangerous to us? | EarthSky.org. Retrieved from https://earthsky.org/space/are-solar-storms-dangerous-to-us

Carreyrou, J. (2019). Bad blood (1st ed.). London: Picador.

Cohan, P. (2018). 6 Warning Signs That Elizabeth Holmes Is Trouble, Says Psychiatrist Who Has Known Her Since Childhood. Retrieved from https://www.inc.com/peter-cohan/6-warning-signs-that-elizabeth-holmes-is-trouble-says-psychiatrist-who-has-known-her-since-childhood.html

Diop, A. (2019). One of Theranos' first investors has learned approximately nothing from its implosion. Retrieved from https://theoutline.com/post/7157/one-of-theranos-first-investors-has-learned-approximately-nothing-from-its-implosion?zd=5&zi=xwc6ouyf

Dunn, T. (2018). Ex-Theranos employee's wife: People like Elizabeth Holmes 'should be in jail'. Retrieved from https://abcnews.go.com/Business/theranos-employees-wife-people-elizabeth-holmes-jail-dropout/story?id=60707423

Flux Biosciences. (2019). Retrieved from https://www.flux.bio/

(Goldberg & Carlson, 2014)

Your Bibliography: Goldberg, J., & Carlson, M. (2014). Parents' Relationship Quality and Children's Behavior in Stable Married and Cohabiting Families. Journal Of Marriage And Family, 76(4), 762-777. doi: 10.1111/jomf.12120

Henning, P. (2019). Elizabeth Holmes's Possible Defense in Theranos Case: Put the Government on Trial. Retrieved from https://www.nytimes.com/2019/05/08/business/dealbook/elizabeth-holmes-theranos-trial.html

Jagannathan, M. (2019). Theranos whistle blower: How to prevent another $600M Silicon Valley disaster. Retrieved from https://www.marketwatch.com/story/theranos-whistleblower-i-was-so-paranoid-about-theranos-and-them-spying-on-me-2019-05-15

Kenton, W. (2019). Free Cash Flow (FCF). Retrieved from https://www.investopedia.com/terms/f/freecashflow.asp

Mezrich, B. (2009). The Accidental Billionaires. Westminster: Doubleday Books.

Raphael, R. (2019). "Like Theranos, but it works"–health start up Genalyte proves its worth. Retrieved from https://www.fastcompany.com/40574949/like-theranos-but-it-works-health-startup-genalyte-proves-its-worth

Schuster, D. (2019). Family of Elizabeth Holmes' fiancé worry she has 'brainwashed' him: source. Retrieved from https://nypost.com/2019/04/06/family-of-elizabeth-holmes-fiance-worry-she-has-brainwashed-him-source/

Stewart, J. (2018). David Boies Pleads Not Guilty. Retrieved from https://www.nytimes.com/2018/09/21/business/david-boies-pleads-not-guilty.html

The 2015 Pulitzer Prize Winner in Investigative Reporting. (2015). Retrieved from https://www.pulitzer.org/winners/wall-street-journal-staff

THERANOS INC - Historical applications for H1B visa and green card sponsorship applications. (2019). Retrieved from https://www.immihelp.com/employer/THERANOS+INC/399122 6/applications

Trump Taps Elizabeth Holmes to Lead FDA - SynBioBeta. (2018). Retrieved from https://synbiobeta.com/trump-taps-elizabeth-holmes-to-lead-fda/

Zahm, M. (2019). Trump and Elizabeth Holmes both lie but Trump is 'off the scale,' says filmmaker Alex Gibney. Retrieved from https://finance.yahoo.com/news/trump-elizabeth-holmes-alex-gibney-122220047.html

Made in the USA
Las Vegas, NV
11 February 2022

43666701R10100